CHRISTIANITY IN THE COURTROOM

2845 Canby Way
80525

— Leo + Linda 970 213-8158

Other books written by the author:

Taking a Second Look at the Second Coming

Decoding Daniel

Revelation Unraveled

Kingdom Combat

Christianity is a White Collar Job

Tabernacle of Grace

Christ in the Constellations

The Greek New Testament Made Easy (Volumes One and Two)

20 Essential Keys to Effective Bible Study

CHRISTIANITY IN THE COURTROOM

Making A Case For The Faith

LES BRITTINGHAM, B.S., M. DIV.

Xulon Press - Maitland

ABOUT THE AUTHOR

The founder of Manna Resource Institute, Les Brittingham, earned his B.S. at Corban University and his M.Div. at Denver Baptist Theological Seminary, where he majored in biblical languages. Les is a Bible scholar who has taught in various academic settings for over 30 years and was a pastor in the Foursquare Denomination for 15 years.

Bringing a rich academic and pastoral background to his books and seminars, Les has a sincere desire to help people in their understanding and presentation of God's Word.

He lives in Fort Collins, Colorado, with his wife, Linda, and is available to speak to churches and other groups.

If you would like more information on books and seminars, or would like to learn more about the ministry of Manna Resource Institute, you can visit our website at www.mannari.com, contact us by e-mail at lesbmri@q.com, or call 970-213-8158.

Xulon Press
2301 Lucien Way #415
Maitland, FL 32751
407.339.4217
www.xulonpress.com

xulon
PRESS

Printed in the United States of America

Printed in the United States of America.

ISBN-13: 978-1-54560-372-7

TABLE OF CONTENTS

FOREWORD

I am passionate about Jesus Christ and His life-changing offer to all who will embrace Him as personal Savior. It was not always the case with me. For most of my formative years I was an angry, confused, low-achieving and directionless individual headed on the wrong path in life, with little hope for a bright, successful future. But that was about to change in a dramatic way when, in 1963, a wonderful Christian woman named Opal Jeffers asked me if I have ever heard of Jesus' love for me. I responded with a "no". That led her to explain to me the simple gospel message of Jesus coming to earth to give His life for my sin and, if I would invite Him into my life by accepting Christ as my Savior, I would be saved and forgiven of all my sins, with the wonderful prospect of spending eternity with Jesus. She invited me to pray and accept Christ into my heart and make Him my Lord and Savior, which I did. I remember the day very well, for it was on this occasion I memorized the books of the Bible through a song my cousin had learned in Sunday School. This would portend that one day I would spend the rest of my life engaged in teaching the Bible to many diverse groups, as well as writing and publishing numerous books on biblically related topics. Through the years, I have experienced the joy and pains of life and the struggle that comes from being a Christian, but I have never forgotten the day Christ came into my life, and I have never ceased thanking Him for taking this wayward young man and changing him forever.

I found the Lord during the radical 60's, when the counterculture began to question all conventional ways of dealing with life, including traditional approaches to Christianity. As a young person growing up in the San Francisco Bay Area, (where much of the radical cultural upheaval of the 60's really began), I found all of my views and beliefs about God and Christianity challenged by the relevant thinkers of the day, who relegated evangelical Christianity to the realm of the ignorant and naive. I began to wonder whether these intellectual gurus were right; maybe Christianity was a product of myth and delusion. I came to realize that I knew *what* to believe when it came to Christian doctrine, yet I did not know *why* I believed what I did. I am thankful for the works of Francis Schaeffer and other Christian thinkers and apologists who helped me understand why Christianity is the only true hope for modern culture. I have investigated the area of apologetics for over forty years and my studies have led me to the absolute belief and conviction that the Christian faith is not only verifiable, but is totally true in all of its claims and viewpoints. I also believe, with great passion and fervor, the message of Christ and God's forgiving love is the only true hope for a decaying world, immersed in secularism and anti-Christian forces that have positioned man as the center (god) of the universe, placing a weight upon him he cannot successfully hold up under.

This material is written to embolden Christian believers to develop a stronger confidence in their faith and to non-believers and skeptics who are asking honest questions about Christianity; to help them find the same hope and peace I found in Christ over fifty years ago.

Les Brittingham

INTRODUCTION

Most of us love to do things we feel confident in performing. Sharing our Christian faith with our culture is no different. We live in a hostile, confrontational, and non-believing world. Fifty years ago, the average person in America had an appreciation for God, Christ, morals, the Bible, and church. Today most of the world has little understanding of what these terms mean, let alone how they apply to their lives. In the last several decades, we have witnessed a systematic dismantling of what was meaningful and truthful in terms of values and ethics. Relativism and a strong faith in secular science, have all but ousted the supernatural and the God of the Bible from everyday life. Yet, the message of Christianity is still powerful, relevant, and meaningful for the decaying society in which we live. Jesus will always be the same: yesterday, today, and forever. The Bible is contemporary because human nature is a tangled mess and there is an insatiable appetite for the supernatural in our culture. The Bible continues to be the best-selling book year-after-year and, though we may not like some of the cultic, new-age and psychic aspects we see popularly displayed in religion, the presence of such forces indicates that there is a hunger to know a world outside of the physical.

However, something tragic has taken place in the Christian world. The church has often retreated behind walls of isolation and comfort. Instead of taking our message to the culture and challenging our secular world with the truths we believe, we have often retreated in fear behind the walls of the church, like a turtle whose head recedes into its shell. In doing so, we have ceded the arena of religious discussion to the cacophonous voices of secular science, atheism, and relativism which have often reduced mankind as a product of chance and impersonal processes, stripping him of meaning and value.

Without money, political influence, mass numbers, or social acceptance, the first-century church moved into the public square with confidence in the message they preached and they literally changed the world. Yet, the average Christian today lacks the boldness and skill to debate or explain even the key issues of his faith. Conservative Christians are being attacked from all sides. Hollywood mocks people of faith with profane movies while, in the political arena, religious folk are blamed for all of America's ills. Years ago, Christians could speak freely without fear of retribution but today we relate the truths of our faith in a much more hostile and fragile environment.

The story of Christianity was not chronicled in an ivory tower. The move of God, narrated throughout the Scriptures, took place in the real world, in a real time-space dimension. The Bible is not a book of fairy tales made up by some creative mind; it is a record of history and reality. The secular culture of our day needs to be challenged by this viewpoint. However, old evangelistic approaches of figuratively beating people over the head with the Bible, shoving religious tracks in their face with harsh and deriding tones of condemnation, or standing on the sidelines shouting a litany of angry epithets at sinners while holding up acrimonious and judgmental placards, are generally not going to be an effective pathway of leading people to Christ in the modern world. We need a more sensitive and reasonable approach that allows us to build bridges into the minds and hearts of the non-Christian. The Holy Spirit can use these bridges to bring the light of Christ to the non-believer. To do this, we need to be willing to listen to the skeptic, engage him with loving and insightful discussion, and show him that regardless of how he responds to our message, we love and respect him as a person that God loves and for whom Jesus died.

Books on apologetics and the defense of Christianity can often be intellectually weighty and hard for the average person to understand and comprehend. Many who write in this area are usually highly trained in the disciplines of logic, mathematics, philosophy, science, linguistics, literature and world religions. Renowned apologists such as C.S. Lewis are brilliant men who write and discuss these topics on a high level and can often be difficult for many to process. Because of this, I have attempted to bring the technical and intellectual into a readable realm the average person should be able to comprehend and appreciate. Our desire is that the material covered in this book will provide a solid foundation and launching point to delve further into the field of apologetics. So let's begin our journey and discover how wonderful and defensible the Christian message truly is.

CHAPTER 1

CHRISTIANITY IS UNIQUE

Most of the world has the same opinion of religion as they do of vacuum cleaners; if you have seen one, you have seen them all. Somehow, our non-offensive culture would like people to believe that all religions are the same and all roads lead to God and heaven, no matter what shape or form "god" takes. The issue today isn't which religion is more credible or representative of the truth, but how does it make you feel? However, the Christian faith isn't the same as all of the rest. The idea that the panorama of today's religions and faiths are interchangeable like car parts is a satanic deception that has been foisted upon the world for hundreds of years. Christianity has always claimed the primary position above all other religions in the world. Christ is a transcendent leader and His message is uniquely distinguishable from all other religious tenets and creeds. There are many unique aspects of the Christian faith.

Christianity is Unique in its Claims

The Bible is unabashed in making bold claims of Christianity's distinctiveness in a number of areas.

The God of the Bible claims to be the only true God

The God of Scripture has declared often and unequivocally that He is the only true God and will not tolerate rivals. He demands an exclusive place for homage and worship from His followers. This is expressed in the Ten Commandments and other places.

> *You shall have no other gods before me. You shall not make for yourself an idol in the form of anything in heaven above or on the earth beneath or in the waters below. You shall not bow down to them or worship them; for I, the LORD your God, am a jealous God....* Exodus 20:3-5

> *You were shown these things so that you might know that the LORD is God; besides him there is no other.* Deuteronomy 4:35

> *But the LORD is the true God; he is the living God, the eternal King. When he is angry, the earth trembles; the nations cannot endure his wrath. Tell them this: "These gods, who did not make the heavens and the earth, will perish from the earth and from under the heavens."* Jeremiah 10:10-11

In spite of what modern culture might proclaim, there is only one true God: Jehovah of the Bible.

Christ claims to be the only way to God

The popular and fashionable idea in our modern religious viewpoint is that there are many roads which lead to God and many pathways to salvation. The Bible contradicts this by stating unambiguously there is only one way to God: Jesus Christ.

> *Therefore Jesus said again, "I tell you the truth, I am the gate for the sheep. All who ever came before me were thieves and robbers, but the sheep did not listen to them. I am the gate; whoever enters through me will be saved. He will come in and go out, and find pasture. The thief comes only to steal and kill and destroy; I have come that they may have life, and have it to the full."* John 10:7-10

> *Jesus answered, "I am the way and the truth and the life. No one comes to the Father except through me."* John 14:6

> *Salvation is found in no one else, for there is no other name under heaven given to men by which we must be saved.* Acts 4:12

The Bible is declared as the only true revelation from God

Throughout its pages, the Bible makes it clear that it is truly a revelation from God and a collaborative effort between God and human authors. Thus, in comparison to all other religious documents, it stands alone in its authority, integrity, and power.

> *To the law and to the testimony! If they do not speak according to this word, they have no light of dawn.* Isaiah 8:20

> *Jesus answered, "It is written: Man does not live on bread alone, but on every word that comes from the mouth of God."* Matthew 4:4

All Scripture is God-breathed and is useful for teaching, rebuking, correcting and training in righteousness, so that the man of God may be thoroughly equipped for every good work. 2 Timothy 3:16-17

Above all, you must understand that no prophesy of Scripture came about by the prophet's own interpretation. For prophecy never had its origin in the will of man, but men spoke from God as they were carried along by the Holy Spirit. 2 Peter 1:20-21

Christianity is Unique in its Historical and Objective Setting

The span of time and geography covered by the story of Judeo-Christian history is amazing in itself.

Numerous civilizations and world rulers

Christianity, with its roots in Judaism chronicled in both Old and New Testaments, encompasses many civilizations and powerful world rulers. From Abraham in Ur of the Chaldees and the great king Nebuchadnezzar of Babylon, to Rome and her powerful Caesars, the Bible chronicles over 2,000 years of world history, culminating in the arrival of Jesus Christ, the Son of God. No other religion can claim this breath of historical interaction.

Several continents and geographical reference points
The Bible was written on three major continents: Asia, Africa and Europe. Contained in its pages are references to hundreds of cities and geographical locations which would be too numerous to delineate. This includes an abundance of rivers, deserts, mountains and historical sites. Jesus was much more than a teacher; He was also a historical person who traveled to specific geographical locations, encountered unique individuals, and performed miracles and fetes surpassing any other human being in history. If the facts of history are not accurate, then the teachings are discredited. Christianity is not a subjective set of ideas to be blindly embraced. Christianity is an objective religion open to verification and documentation.

The God of Christianity is Unique in His Character and Power

The God of Christianity is unique in His person, power, and presence. No god in any other religion possesses the characteristics and personal qualities we see in the God of the Bible. Here are some aspects which distinguish Jehovah God from all others:

God is the Creator of the universe
From the beginning of the Bible, God is established as the Creator of the universe. Later, John amplifies this by stating that the preincarnate Christ was also involved in this process as well.

> *In the beginning God created the heavens and the earth.* Genesis 1:1

The God who made the world and everything in it is the Lord of heaven and earth and does not live in temples built by hands. Acts 17:24

In the beginning was the Word, and the Word was with God, and the Word was God. He was with God in the beginning. Through him all things were made; without him nothing was made that has been made. John 1:1-3

God is one in essence but triune in personality

The God of Christianity is unique in its concept of the *trinity*: One God in essence with three personalities. This is first indicated in the book of Genesis with the use of the pronoun *us*:

Then God said, "Let us make man in our image, in our likeness, and let them rule over the fish of the sea and the birds of the air, over the livestock, over all the earth, and over all the creatures that move along the ground." Genesis 1:26

Later, the New Testament attributes deity to Jesus and the Holy Spirit:

In the beginning was the Word [Jesus], and the Word was with God, and the Word was God. John 1:1

Then Peter said, "Ananias, how is it that Satan has so filled your heart that you have lied to the Holy Spirit and have kept for yourself some of the

> *money you received for the land?.... You have not lied to men but to God."* Acts 5:3-4

This triune aspect of God is exclusive to the Judeo-Christian God. These three persons are active throughout the pages of the Holy Scriptures and in the world today. In fact, Jesus equates the personalities as God by suggesting baptism be performed in three names:

> *Therefore go and make disciples of all nations, baptizing them in the name of the Father and of the Son and of the Holy Spirit.* Matthew 28:19

God desires covenantal relationship with mankind

The God of the Bible is also unique in that He desires covenantal relationship with His creation. In biblical times, covenants between individuals (as well as nations) were the common ways of establishing bonds of trust and relationships. These covenants were binding and the terms of the covenants were expected to be followed and adhered to without exception. The Lord seeks the same communal relationship with His human creation that He possesses in the trinity. This is demonstrated many times in the Scriptures and vividly portrayed in the life of Abraham, Israel, and the church:

> *On that day the LORD made a covenant with Abram and said, "To your descendants I give this land, from the river of Egypt to the great river, the Euphrates."* Genesis 15:18

> *Now if you obey me fully and keep my covenant, then out of all nations you will be my treasured*

> *possession. Although the whole earth is mine, you will be for me a kingdom of priests and a holy nation. These are the words you are to speak to the Israelites.* Exodus 19:5-6
>
> *In the same way, after supper he took the cup, saying, "This cup is the new covenant in my blood; do this, whenever you drink it, in remembrance of me."* 1 Corinthians 11:25

God is love and extends this love to His creation
One of the most dominant characteristics of God in the Bible is love. The Lord doesn't just possess love, He, by His very nature, is love. God's love is a defining quality in His relationship with His people. This is expressed poignantly in both Old and New Testaments:

> *The LORD did not set his affection on you and choose you because you were more numerous than other peoples, for you were the fewest of all peoples. But it was because the LORD loved you and kept the oath he swore to your forefathers that he brought you out with a mighty hand and redeemed you from the land of slavery, from the power of Pharaoh king of Egypt. Know therefore that the LORD your God is God; he is the faithful God, keeping his covenant of love to a thousand generations of those who love him and keep his commands.* Deuteronomy 7:7-9
>
> *And so we know and rely on the love God has for us. God is love. Whoever lives in love lives in God, and God in him.* 1 John 4:16

Again, most religions of the world never speak of their gods in these terms. Love is a unique characteristic of Jehovah.

God is personal, relational, and communicative

The God of Christianity is unique in His quality of desiring personal communication with His creation. There are dozens of times in the Scriptures where the Lord is depicted as talking and dialoging with individuals and leaders. We witness this early in the book of Genesis and many other times in the Bible:

> *The LORD God took the man and put him in the Garden of Eden to work it and take care of it. And the LORD God commanded the man, "You are free to eat from any tree in the garden; but you must not eat from the tree of the knowledge of good and evil, for when you eat of it you will surely die." The LORD God said, "It is not good for the man to be alone. I will make a helper suitable for him."* Genesis 2:15-18

> *The LORD said, "Throw it on the ground." Moses threw it on the ground and it became a snake, and he ran from it. Then the LORD said to him, "Reach out your hand and take it by the tail." So Moses reached out and took hold of the snake and it turned back into a staff in his hand.* Exodus 4:3-4

The greatest demonstration of God speaking to His creation was through the person of Jesus Christ. He is called the very *Word* of God:

> *In the beginning was the Word, and the Word was with God, and the Word was God.* John 1:1

Christianity is Unique in its Founder - Jesus Christ

Not only is the God of Christianity unique, so is its founder. Jesus Christ is the most distinguished human being and religious leader in history. He is distinctive in His character, claims, and conduct. There are many attributes that make Jesus Christ stand apart from all other religious leaders:

His prophesied birth

Jesus' ancestry and birthplace were clearly predicted hundreds of years ahead of time and fulfilled to the letter in His life.

Lineage from Jesse

> *A shoot will come up from the stump of Jesse; from his roots a Branch will bear fruit. The Spirit of the LORD will rest on him—the Spirit of wisdom and of understanding, the Spirit of counsel and of power, the Spirit of knowledge and of the fear of the LORD.* Isaiah 11:1-2

> *Now Jesus... the son of Jesse, the son of Obed, the son of Boaz, the son of Salmon, the son of Nahshon....* Luke 3:23, 32

Birthplace in Bethlehem

> *But you, Bethlehem Ephrathah, though you are small among the clans of Judah, out of you will come for me one who will be ruler over Israel, whose origins are from of old, from ancient times.* Micah 5:2

> *After Jesus was born in Bethlehem in Judea, during the time of King Herod, Magi from the east came to Jerusalem.* Matthew 2:1

His virgin conception

No human being on the face of the earth has ever been born without the involvement of two human parents. In the case of Jesus, He was conceived without the aid of a human father. This was prophesied in the Old Testament and fulfilled in the New:

> *Therefore the Lord himself will give you a sign: The virgin will be with child and will give birth to a son, and will call him Immanuel.* Isaiah 7:14

> *This is how the birth of Jesus Christ came about: His mother Mary was pledged to be married to Joseph, but before they came together, she was found to be with child through the Holy Spirit.... All this took place to fulfill what the Lord had said through the prophet: "The virgin will be with child and will give birth to a son, and they will call him Immanuel" which means, "God with us." When Joseph woke up, he did what the*

> *angel of the Lord had commanded him and took Mary home as his wife. But he had no union with her until she gave birth to a son. And he gave him the name Jesus.* Matthew 1:18, 22-25

His nature as both God and man

Jesus is not only declared to be God, but also human at the same time. Thus being God, He could represent the offended holy God and, in becoming man, He could represent the sinning offender. He was indeed the God-Man.

> *In the beginning was the Word, and the Word was with God, and the Word was God. He was with God in the beginning.* John 1:1-2

> *Who, being in very nature God, did not consider equality with God something to be grasped, but made himself nothing, taking the very nature of a servant, being made in human likeness. And being found in appearance as a man, he humbled himself and became obedient to death—even death on a cross!* Philippians 2:6-8

His sinless life

For Jesus to die for the sins of the world required that He, Himself, be without sin. This is a characteristic the Bible is unambiguous about:

> *God made him who had no sin to be sin for us, so that in him we might become the righteousness of God.* 2 Corinthians 5:21

For we do not have a high priest who is unable to sympathize with our weaknesses, but we have one who has been tempted in every way, just as we are—yet was without sin. Hebrews 4:15

His ability to heal

Jesus' prolific demonstration of healing and restoration of the human condition was a major force in His ministry. No one in recorded history possessed the prowess to heal with such miraculous power and frequency:

Jesus went throughout Galilee, teaching in their synagogues, preaching the good news of the kingdom, and healing every disease and sickness among the people. Matthew 4:23

When Jesus had called the Twelve together, he gave them power and authority to drive out all demons and to cure diseases, and he sent them out to preach the kingdom of God and to heal the sick. Luke 9:1-2

His power to raise the dead

On several occasions Jesus raised individuals from the dead. The most dramatic demonstration of this was the raising of Lazarus out of the grave he had lain in for four days:

Jesus, once more deeply moved, came to the tomb. It was a cave with a stone laid across the entrance. "Take away the stone," he said. "But, Lord," said Martha, the sister of the dead man, "by this time

> *there is a bad odor, for he has been there four days." Then Jesus said, "Did I not tell you that if you believed, you would see the glory of God?" So they took away the stone. Then Jesus looked up and said, "Father, I thank you that you have heard me. I knew that you always hear me, but I said this for the benefit of the people standing here, that they may believe that you sent me." When he had said this, Jesus called in a loud voice, "Lazarus, come out!" The dead man came out, his hands and feet wrapped with strips of linen, and a cloth around his face. Jesus said to them, "Take off the grave clothes and let him go."*
> John 11:38-44

His control over nature

One of the most incredible aspects of Jesus life and ministry was His ability to control the very forces of nature that He created. He accomplished fetes in this arena that no human religious leader has ever been able to match. Whether it was turning the water into wine, walking on the water or controlling gale forced winds on the Sea of Galilee, Jesus was the master of nature.

> *Jesus said to the servants, "Fill the jars with water"; so they filled them to the brim. Then he told them, "Now draw some out and take it to the master of the banquet." They did so and the master of the banquet tasted the water that had been turned into wine. He did not realize where it had come from, though the servants who had drawn the water knew. Then he called the bridegroom aside and said, "Everyone brings out the*

> *choice wine first and then the cheaper wine after the guests have had too much to drink; but you have saved the best till now."* John 2:7-10

> *During the fourth watch of the night Jesus went out to them, walking on the lake. When the disciples saw him walking on the lake, they were terrified. "It's a ghost," they said, and cried out in fear. But Jesus immediately said to them: "Take courage! It is I. Don't be afraid."* Matthew 14:25-27

> *He got up, rebuked the wind and said to the waves, "Quiet! Be still!" Then the wind died down and it was completely calm. He said to his disciples, "Why are you so afraid? Do you still have no faith?" They were terrified and asked each other, "Who is this? Even the wind and the waves obey him!"* Mark 4:39-41

His authority over Satan

From the beginning of His ministry Jesus made it clear that His greatest enemy was not Rome, but Satan (better known as the devil). Every time Jesus encountered demonic forces from hell, He dominated them with overcoming strength and authority, proving His superiority over the evil kingdom of Satan:

> *Jesus knew their thoughts and said to them, "Every kingdom divided against itself will be ruined, and every city or household divided against itself will not stand. If Satan drives out Satan, he is divided against himself. How*

> *then can his kingdom stand? And if I drive out demons by Beelzebub, by whom do your people drive them* out? *So then, they will be your judges. But if I drive out demons by the Spirit of God, then the kingdom of God has come upon you."* Matthew 12:25-28

> *In the synagogue there was a man possessed by a demon, an evil spirit. He cried out at the top of his voice, "Ha! What do you want with us, Jesus of Nazareth? Have you come to destroy us? I know who you are—the Holy One of God!" "Be quiet!" Jesus said sternly. "Come out of him!" Then the demon threw the man down before them all and came out without injuring him.* Luke 4:33-35

His bodily resurrection

Perhaps the greatest evidence that sets Jesus a part from every other religious leader and truly makes Him unique is the bodily resurrection from the dead. Jesus predicted this would happen and it did. The resurrection of Jesus was the salient component of the witness of the early church.

> *The reason my Father loves me is that I lay down my life—only to take it up again. No one takes it from me, but I lay it down of my own accord. I have authority to lay it down and authority to take it up again. This command I received from my Father.* John 10:17-18

> *By this gospel you are saved, if you hold firmly to the word I preached to you. Otherwise, you have*

believed in vain. For what I received I passed on to you as of first importance: that Christ died for our sins according to the Scriptures, that he was buried, that he was raised on the third day according to the Scriptures, and that he appeared to Peter, and then to the Twelve. After that, he appeared to more than five hundred of the brothers at the same time, most of whom are still living, though some have fallen asleep. Then he appeared to James, then to all the apostles, and last of all he appeared to me also, as to one abnormally born. 1 Corinthians 15:2-8

Christianity is Unique in its Biblical Writings

Most religions have a sacred book they use as the basis of their beliefs and practices. Christianity has the Bible. Much of what makes the Christian faith unique is the incredible nature of the biblical documents contained in what we call the Scriptures.

Unique in continuity and composition

The enormity and scope of the process which has brought us the Holy Bible is almost a miracle in itself. It consists of sixty-six books, written in three languages, on three continents by about forty diverse authors from doctors, kings, farmers and fishermen. They wrote from wildernesses, dungeons, islands and palaces, covering a span of about 2,000 years. These books were inscribed over a period of 1500 years, proving that most of the biblical authors did not know each other or collaborate with one another. Yet they wrote with amazing coherence and purpose to produce a marvelous story and narrative.

In spite of the diversity within its pages, the Bible has an amazing sense of accuracy, unity, and incredible themes which offer hope for mankind in every area of life. Among the millions of books which have been penned over the years, there is nothing comparable to the Bible, nor will there ever be.

Unique in prophesying events hundreds of years in advance

The Bible stands alone in its ability to forecast and prophesy events and civilizations hundreds of years ahead of time. There is no book or individual that possesses the ability to see into the future as the biblical writings.

Jesus Christ

In regards to Christ alone, there are over *three hundred* prophecies in the Old Testament about Him that were fulfilled in the New Testament. These topics range from His birth, ancestry, death, resurrection and much more. We will discuss some of these later under our treatment of Jesus Christ. Keep in mind many of the prophecies of the Old Testament were written hundreds of years before the birth of Christ.

Daniel

One of the most striking examples of biblical prognostication comes from the book of Daniel. Scholarship has confirmed that Daniel was indeed a sixth-century BC prophet, who chronicled his book while living in Babylon during the seventy year captivity mentioned in Jeremiah. Daniel's prescience is uncanny as he forecasts several civilizations hundreds of years ahead of his time. Here are some of the prophetic forecasts we find in Daniel:

1. Daniel interprets Nebuchadnezzar's dream of the statue as four consecutive world dominating empires starting with Babylon (Daniel 2:36-43). We know this is exactly what happened historically as Babylon was followed by the empires of the Medes and Persians, Greece, and the Roman Empire.

2. In Daniel 7, we are told the prophet received a vision of four intimidating and frightening beasts: a lion, bear, leopard, and a terrifying creature. This vision corresponds with the dream of Nebuchadnezzar earlier. The detailed descriptions of these four beast match the nature of Babylon, the Medes and Persians, Greece and Rome.

3. Daniel experiences a vision in chapter 8 of a two-horned ram and a goat with a prominent horn, which is interpreted as Media and Persia and Greece:

   The two-horned ram that you saw represents the kings of Media and Persia. The shaggy goat is the king of Greece, and the large horn between his eyes is the first king. Daniel 8:20-21

   What is so amazing about this text is that the Medes and Persians did not conquer Babylon until 539 BC and Greece did not become a prominent power until the fourth-century BC. The large horn is an obvious reference to Alexander the Great who conquered most of the world by 326 BC. Daniel in essence is prophesying detailed events 200 years ahead of his time.

4. The most amazing example of Daniel's prophetical prowess is in Daniel 11, where Daniel projects dozens of events, rulers, and details of history from around 529 BC to 168 BC, which include the Medes and Persians, Alexander the Great, the Ptolemy's of Egypt and the emergence of the ruthless Seleucid King Antiochus Epiphanes IV, who desecrated and defiled the temple in Jerusalem in 168 BC.

There is no other explanation for this incredible and accurate forecast of history than a supernatural influence behind the biblical records.

Unique in its distribution

The Bible has been the best-selling book in the world for hundreds of years. It has virtually been translated in every known language. Even today, many organizations are actively working on translating the Bible into new dialects. The Cambridge History of the Bible states, "No other book has known anything approaching this constant circulation." (*Cambridge History of the Bible*, p. 479)

Unique in its longevity
The survival of the Bible is simply an astonishing fact, which testifies to its unique nature. Josh McDowell states:

> *Being written on material that perishes, having to be copied and recopied for hundreds of years before the invention of the printing press, did not diminish its style, correctness nor existence. The Bible, compared with other ancient writings, has more manuscript evidence than any 10 pieces of classical literature combined.* (Josh McDowell. *Evidence That Demands A Verdict*, p. 19)

The Bible has survived through times of countless persecutions and attempts to eradicate it from the earth. Voltaire, the French philosopher, said that:

> *In one hundred years from his time Christianity would be swept from existence and passed into history.* (Sidney Collet in *All About the Bible*, cited by Josh McDowell in *Evidence That Demands A Verdict*, p. 20)

Well, Voltaire is dead and the Bible, with its Christian message, continues to abound in circulation. It is also interesting to note that 50 years after his death, the Geneva Bible Society used his press and house to reproduce stacks of Bibles. For hundreds of years, the Bible has also withstood constant attacks and incessant criticism directed at impugning its accuracy. However, the disciplines of archaeology and textual criticism continues to affirm the veracity and accuracy of the Biblical truths, while silencing its critics.

Christianity is unique and stands alone in its claims and its evidence. It is one thing to make assertions and another thing to back them up with facts. The following discussion is designed to help strengthen our ability to defend these unique qualities of our faith in the midst of a world that has grown increasingly skeptical of and cynical toward Christianity, and those who espouse its claims.

CHAPTER 2

APOLOGETICS: THE ART OF DEFENSE

Defending the Christian faith is commonly referred to as *apologetics*. It is important that we understand not only what apologetics is, but also why it is important for Christians to defend their belief system in the face of virulent criticism and hostile attacks from those in our culture, who oppose Christianity. When Scripture is studied thoroughly in this area, we will find that standing up for our faith is a task which all believers can and should embrace.

What Is Apologetics?

The Greek word *apologia*, from which we derive the term *apologetics*, means *to defend* or *answer*. Apologetics is the aspect of Christian evangelism that appeals to the mind by defending the key issues of the faith and answering questions raised by skeptics and honest seekers of truth. Peter, in his epistle, admonishes all believers to be prepared to give an answer for the hope that is within them:

> *But in your hearts set apart Christ as Lord. Always be prepared to give an answer to everyone*

> *who asks you to give the reason for the hope that you have. But do this with gentleness and respect....* 1 Peter 3:15

Many people harbor legitimate doubts about the credibility of Christianity and often express misconceptions regarding the Christian faith. Providing sensible answers helps to address their concerns so that the individual has an unobstructed path toward a clear understanding of the Gospel of Christ. We should not be deceived or deluded into thinking that providing evidence and reason will automatically bring people to the Lord. Salvation is still a matter of faith in the heart and the convicting work of the Holy Spirit. However, we might liken apologetics to a car traveling on a road filled with potholes. If we eliminate the potholes, the car has a better chance of reaching its destination. Answering questions clearly and accurately can potentially eliminate some of the potholes in human thought and perception regarding Christianity. The truth of the resurrection of Christ may be obvious to those of us who have embraced Him, but it may not be so clear to the modern skeptic who believes that miracles cannot happen, thus precluding the resurrection from ever occurring historically.

Why Defend Our Faith?

Since we know what apologetics is, it is appropriate to ask the question, "Why is it necessary to make a defense for Christianity?" There are several reasons why a defense of our faith is essential.

Christianity is founded on bold claims

Christianity is undergirded by bold claims that need to be backed up. There are many religions in our world and each of them, in one way or another, claims a corner on the truth in both the temporal and eternal arenas. They cannot all be right; it is not possible for all roads to lead to God. Historically, Christianity has positioned itself as a higher authority over all other religions. Jesus Christ had no qualms in asserting that He was the only way to God. Someone once said, "It is not bragging if you can back it up."

Christians are narrow-minded in their belief that Christianity is the only true pathway to God and salvation. We are this way because Jesus was narrow-minded about Himself. Often we will be asked, "Do you think that your way is the only way to God?" This is a set-up question. If we say, "no," we allow any old religion to suffice, but if we say, "yes," we relegate the Muslims, Hindus, or any other religion espousing a conflicting view of Christianity to an inferior position. This can come across as very unfair and arrogant. However, the Bible is unequivocal in its declaration that true biblical Christianity is the only valid way to God. Jesus and the writers of Scripture made bold claims in this area:

Jesus proclaimed He was the only way to God

Jesus made it clear that He was the only way to God. He emphatically declared that the only means to have a relationship with the Father was through Him. If Jesus was so emphatic in this area, then His followers should be as well. Jesus was attacked and challenged for His narrow assertions but He could back them up. Notice what He said concerning Himself:

> *Jesus answered, "I am the way and the truth and the life. No one comes to the Father except through me."* John 14:6

Every time Jesus mentions the phrase, *I am,* He used an intense form in the Greek, *ego eimi*. This can be translated, *I and only I am*. The message in this verse could not be clearer: Jesus is the only way to Father God. This phraseology is abundant in the New Testament and brings focus to the fact that Jesus is unique among all others.

Jesus also incorporated a shepherd's analogy in another place to emphasize that He was the only valid gate for the sheep:

> *Therefore Jesus said again, "I tell you the truth, I am the gate for the sheep. All who ever came before me were thieves and robbers, but the sheep did not listen to them. I am the gate; whoever enters through me will be saved. He will come in and go out, and find pasture."* John 10:7-9

Our Lord makes it plain that anyone who tries to enter God's sheepfold by some way besides Him is following the wrong path and coming through the wrong gate. Many claim to be the way to God but Jesus is the only true gate to God's throne and presence.

Peter affirmed that Jesus was the only way to God

The apostle Peter was a first-century, first-hand witness to many of the things that Jesus said and did. He himself was once skeptical of Christ: denied Him three times and fled in fear of the Romans. Something happened to transform Peter - he met the resurrected Jesus. Notice how Peter boldly and unequivocally proclaimed Christ as the only way to God.

> *Salvation is found in no one else, for there is no other name under heaven given to men by which we must be saved.* Acts 4:12

Paul declared Jesus Christ as the only valid gospel

We know from reading the book of Acts that at one time Paul, formerly known as Saul, was an archenemy of Christ and a rabid persecutor of the church. But his attitude suddenly changes when he was dramatically confronted by Jesus on the Damascus road, while on his way to throw some believers into prison. Paul's life was miraculously altered through an encounter with Christ. Paul fervently declares the good news (gospel) of Christ was the only valid gospel of salvation.

> *I am astonished that you are so quickly deserting the one who called you by the grace of Christ and are turning to a different gospel—which is really no gospel at all. Evidently some people are throwing you into confusion and are trying to pervert the gospel of Christ. But even if we or an angel from heaven should preach a gospel other than the one we preached to you, let him be eternally condemned! As we have already said,*

> *so now I say again: if anybody is preaching to you a gospel other than what you accepted, let him be eternally condemned!* Galatians 1:6-9

All religions possess credible moral teachings, valid precepts, and admirable qualities. What we are talking about is the nature of salvation, mankind's relationship with his God, the forgiveness of sins because of Christs' work on the cross, and our eternal state. If Christianity is going to make bold claims of superiority, the claims must be defended.

Christianity is the only hope for a decaying culture

We need to defend the Christian faith not only because of its bold claims but also because, without the principles of Christianity in a society, mankind faces severe and dire consequences. The bed rock of Western Civilization for hundreds of years has been Judeo-Christian principles and ethics, particularly expressed in the Ten Commandments. Our country was founded on a healthy respect for God, the Bible, and Christian principles. Unfortunately, today we are witnessing the erosion of these principles, while suffering the devastating and destructive results of secularism on our culture. Because of society's rejection of Judeo-Christian values, human life has been devalued. Subjects like late-term abortions, euthanasia and assisted suicide demonstrate how the value of life has taken on less importance in our secular society. Wherever morals and a strong belief in God wane in a culture, there will always be a proportional amount of social ills to be dealt with. Judeo-Christian ethics have always been important elements in our culture towards establishing solid morals and values. The scholarly apologist, John Warwick Montgomery, in his tape series, *Sensible Christianity*, demonstrates how the last three centuries have led to the decay of Western civilization.

In the eighteenth century (1700's), the Bible was killed

Until the latter part of the eighteenth century, there was still a respect for religion and the Bible. In most of the European countries, God was associated with the monarchy, and Europe was experiencing deep dissatisfaction with this relationship. The eighteenth century witnessed the rise of the Enlightenment Movement dominated by the French philosophers. They were convinced that a moral society could emerge apart from biblical revelation. These philosophers maintained that man could be the answer to his own culture and that human reason would replace biblical authority.

However, the French Revolution, with its slaughter of human life, should have demonstrated the folly of this optimistic view of man. This approach to life also crept into the United States in the form of *deism* which taught that after completing His creation, God abandoned it and allowed nature to take its course through natural law. Natural law was becoming more relevant and important to society than biblical revelation. Many of the founders of the United States were deists, (e.g., Thomas Jefferson and Ben Franklin). In the eighteenth century, human reason subtly replaced biblical authority. Some of this change in belief is hard to detect, since in the eighteenth century one had to use Christian terms and phraseology to be accepted and read. The authority of human reason, apart from biblical revelation, was now firmly in place. One could say that the Bible was killed.

In the nineteenth century (1800's), God was killed

Without respect for biblical authority, the next step would be to kill God. In the nineteenth century the, *God-is-dead movement* arose. After biblical authority is cast off, there is nothing to stop man from usurping the role of God and replacing Him. Natural explanations for the origins of life came on the scene in such works as *The Origin of Species* by Charles Darwin. The world was ripe to find a way to explain the meaning of life without the supernatural. Rushdoony comments on this:

> *When the first edition of Charles Darwin's ON THE ORIGIN OF SPECIES was published on November 24, 1859, all 1,250 copies sold out on the day of publication. The world was waiting for a theory with scientific prestige to render the Bible and God obsolete, and men immediately jumped on the bandwagon of Darwinism. George Bernard Shaw described the relief of men at being rid of God and declared "the world jumped at Darwin."* (R. J. Rushdoony. *The Necessity for Creationism* [pamphlet], p. 1)

In this century, the German philosopher Nietzsche popularized the notion that God was dead. Nietzsche's famous doctrine, *nihilism*, which is a rejection of the Christian view of morality and religion, was based on his view that God was dead. Nietzsche's viewpoints would later have tremendous influence on Hitler as he established the state as more important than morality. The world was about to pay a severe price for this departure from God. The twentieth century would bring to fruition the consequences of having cast out the Bible and God from our thinking.

In the twentieth century (1900's), man was killed

When we come to the twentieth century, the world will suffer the effects of man's attempts to cast the Bible and God out of his everyday life. Two world wars; the terrible holocaust of the Jews as well as numerous holocausts which have followed; the Korean and Vietnam conflicts; the rise of communism, fascism, and Nazism; and the decline of Western civilization represent the result of man's desire to carry on without God and the standards of Judeo-Christian ethics. The result of these events have recorded the untold killing and maiming of millions all over the world.

The twentieth century also gave us rampant genocide and the unprecedented destruction of our children on many continents, while the twenty-first century has given rise to virulent strains of terrorism which has wreaked havoc and death everywhere. Today, our society is like a spoke trying to find meaning without a wheel. Mankind searches for significance without acknowledging the God Who created him and the task is impossible. It was C.S. Lewis who once described mankind's attempt to find meaning without God as "demanding the function and removing the organ." When there is a departure from biblical viewpoints, mankind always suffers.

The last hundred years has witnessed some of the most hideous treatments of mankind the world has ever known. Victor Frankl, an Auschwitz survivor, has been able to go beyond the surface and analyze why Hitler and his minions were able to kill so many people without remorse. Frankl put it this way:

> *If we present man with a concept of man which is not true, we may well corrupt him. When we present him as an automation of reflexes, as a mind machine, as a bundle of instincts, as a pawn of drive and reactions, as a mere product of heredity and environment, we feed the nihilism to which modern man is, in any case, prone. I became acquainted with the last stage of corruption in my second concentration camp, Auschwitz. The gas chambers of Auschwitz were the ultimate consequence of the theory that man is nothing but the product of heredity and environment—or, as the Nazis liked to say, "of blood and soil." I am absolutely convinced that the gas chambers of Auschwitz, Treblinka, and Maidanek were ultimately prepared not in some ministry or other in Berlin, but rather at the desks and in lecture halls of nihilistic scientists and philosophers.* (Victor Frankl in *The Doctor and the Soul*, cited by Ravi Zecharias in *Can Man Live Without God?*, p. 25)

We are a very educated society

Another reason it is important for Christians to be able to defend their faith in modern culture is that our society is becoming increasingly more educated, requiring thoughtful and intelligent answers to their questions. Many have attended and graduated from colleges and universities where Judeo-Christian values are ridiculed and attacked. People today are more apt to question what is true than they were in previous generations. In the past, an individual would most likely continue to attend the church denomination in which they grew up and adhere to the religious convictions of their parents, but that is no longer the case. Christians are often defined by the intellectual elites as gullible, naive, stupid, and easily duped with very little to offer the world in terms of an intelligent discussion. This is not true. Some of the most intelligent people in history have been committed followers of Jesus Christ, e.g., Paul, Augustine, Handel, C. S. Lewis, and Francis Schaeffer to name a few. Christian thinkers from all academic disciplines, whether medicine, science, mathematics, aerospace, philosophy, or economics have made great impacts upon our society.

The reality is that modern man has been so deluged with secular thinking that he no longer has room for Christianity or the God of Scripture in his worldview. We need to be prepared to answer honest questions asked by the legitimate seekers of truth. If Christians do not know how to defend their own beliefs, they only reinforce the culture's view of their inadequacies and gullibility. As a result, they will be ineffective in challenging the skeptic's criticism about the validity of their faith. Many Christians are apprehensive about an approach to the secular world that involves persuasion or argumentation. At times, we feel more comfortable with an easier route to evangelism that requires little thought or scholarship. Here are a couple of dominant philosophies we will face in our culture as we defend our faith.

Secularism

Secularism attempts to explain the world, life, and origins apart from God/theism. Over the years, our public schools have systematically drifted away from a God-centered universe to a materialistic-centered universe. A good illustration of this viewpoint is the theory of evolution or classic Darwinism. This viewpoint in general rejects a theistic world, attempting to explain origins through a natural process. In the 1920's, a famous trial took place famously known as the Scope's trial because a substitute biology teacher by the name of Scopes taught the theory of evolution in one of his classes. By so doing, he violated a Tennessee law that forbade this teaching. The trial ended in the conviction of Scopes in spite of the fact that his lawyer, Clarence Darrow, by all accounts, solidly defeated the prosecutor William Jennings Bryan. How things have changed! In today's world, one is ridiculed if he maintains a belief that God created the world and a teacher would be reprimanded severely if he unashamedly taught such a belief in the public school system.

Secularism does not allow for miracles or the supernatural in its understanding of the universe. It presents mankind as the product of chance and random experiences. He has no personal God to relate to and is forced to find meaning apart from the Creator. Since Christianity is a religion based on the existence of a supernatural God, secularism has little use for Christianity.

Relativity

Another powerful force in our society which undermines Judeo-Christian thinking is the philosophy of *relativity*. Relativity denies the existence of absolute truth. Since man determines what is right and wrong, he has no standard but himself by which to judge truth and set the standards of morality. This is in contrast to Christianity which is rooted in absolutes, particularly moral absolutes that emanate from a Holy God. Because of the relativistic nature of our society, it is difficult for anyone to talk about anything in absolute terms. It is like trying to nail Jell-O to a tree. Man does what pleases him, which leads to a very selfish approach to life and its problems. The mantra is, "If it feels good, do it." Without an immutable outside force determining the value system, man decides what is right or wrong even at the expense of human life. Hitler decided who was worthy to live and who should die. The poor, the handicapped, and the Jews were deemed expendable. There was no moral restraint. Without rights and wrongs that are immutable, who could challenge Hitler in regard to his abhorrent behavior? This is why the message of Christianity is all the more important.

We cannot have a value system that continually changes with the whims and vagaries of culture and modern thinking. Once we change the rules, we have changed the game. Hitler changed the rules and therefore, he changed the game, a game none of us liked.

What is Our Approach to Apologetics?

Skeptics and critics have a way of separating Christianity from the real world. They often depict the Christian faith as a fairy tale detached from the norms of life. To them, the Bible is an outdated ancient book created by dreamers and enchanters, cooked up in many remote places and detached from reality. Christians are viewed as duped and mindless, while the secular world has claimed a corner on the market in logic, facts, truth, and reason. Our apologetics approach in defending our faith is simply: *to persuade the unbeliever to consider Christianity in terms that he can understand and in ways he processes other aspects of his life.*

We desire the unbeliever to evaluate the Christian faith in the same way he analyzes other areas and dimensions in his life. For instance, if a man is convinced that Abraham Lincoln gave the Gettysburg Address, he uses certain processes to come to this conclusion. Historical research is one of these disciplines. Therefore, it is logical that one would use historical research to verify the existence of Jesus. Many people assume that Christians have taken a blind leap in their faith and only believe in Christianity because they need a crutch or it makes them feel good, not because it makes sense or is even true. Most of the things in life we believe in and practice have been accepted as the result of common sense and logic. Why should the Christian faith be any different? If a man rejects Christ, let it be solely because of his *heart* and not his *head.*

What Results Might We Expect?

Defending our faith in the modern world has its risks. Here are some of the reactions and results we can expect if we defend our faith to our world.

We will irritate some

The teachings and tenets of Christianity can be very offensive to some. The Christian message is so radical, so distinct, and so penetrating that its claims perturb many who would rather live comfortable lives in their selfish and secular viewpoints. The gospel message is often diametrically opposed to the philosophies of the world and the emptiness of vain religion. Many are reluctant to defend or share their faith because they do not want to offend others who might differ with them. Our culture is influenced by a let's-all-get-along philosophy that views conflict and offending people as abhorrent. This "politically correct" approach has replaced truth with good feelings and watered down beliefs and convictions. Because of this attitude, Christians are often intimidated about sharing their faith because they do not want to be described as parochial and judgmental.

We will never preach the gospel effectively if our ultimate goal is to get along with and to be liked by everyone. By their nature, the gospel of Christ and the essential message of Christianity are offensive. Subjects like personal sin, the rebellion of mankind, and eternal judgment are not topics that elicit joy and glee in the modern world. The message of Christianity declares that there is something wrong with man, an idea that does not harmonize with a culture that has made man a "god". The Bible speaks of the offensive nature of the gospel and warns us of potential negative consequences:

> *...but we preach Christ crucified: a stumbling block to Jews and foolishness to Gentiles.* 1 Corinthians1:23

> *All men will hate you because of me, but he who stands firm to the end will be saved.* Matthew10:22

> *Then you will be handed over to be persecuted and put to death, and you will be hated by all nations because of me.* Matthew 24:9

The gospel gets in the way of a world with a mindset that wants to do things its own way. We see an example of this fact in Paul's encounter with the city of Ephesus. His preaching and effectiveness in persuading the worshippers of Artemis that Jesus is Lord, was cutting into the lucrative idol business of the local merchants. The frenzied crowd acted with hostility to the preaching of Paul:

> *He called them together, along with the workmen in related trades, and said: "Men, you know we receive a good income from this business. And you see and hear how this fellow Paul has convinced and led astray large numbers of people here in Ephesus and in practically the whole province of Asia. He says that man-made gods are no gods at all. There is danger not only that our trade will lose its good name, but also that the temple of the great goddess...." When they heard this, they were furious and began shouting: "Great is Artemis of the Ephesians!" Soon the whole city was in an uproar. The people seized Gaius and Aristarchus, Paul's traveling companions from Macedonia, and rushed as one man into the theater.* Acts 19:25-29

Paul and his friends were seized and abused by the angry crowd. To be a defender of the faith and challenge the world with the claims of Christ, will not always endear us to our audience. However, the good news is that some will receive and embrace the Lord after hearing the message.

This is what makes defending our faith worthwhile and rewarding.

We will influence some

One result of defending our faith is that we will offend some. The other result is that we will potentially influence many with the powerful message of Christ. Christianity was birthed in a hostile environment with the odds stacked against its success. The renowned scholar F. F. Bruce, in his classic book, *The Defence [sic] of the Gospel*, discusses four intimidating and formidable enemies of Christianity the early church had to face and defeat, for it to have the effect it did upon the world:

1.) *Judaism* – The leadership of Israel, even after the resurrection of Christ, continued to oppose and resist this new religion founded upon the life of Christ. In fact, a pivotal event in the book of Acts that reflected this hostile attitude of the Jews was the stoning of Stephen recorded in Acts 7, followed later by the persecution of the church in Jerusalem which caused it to scatter. In city after city, the Jewish leadership remained hostile to this new message of the early church. In spite of this, the gospel continued to have a powerful impact in many of these cities.

2.) *Paganism* – Paganism, with its worship of numerous gods, gaudy temples, and pagan practices rooted in the culture of the Greek cities of Asia Minor and Macedonia, was also a formidable opponent of the Christian message. The book of Acts records hostile confrontations in cities like Lystra, Ephesus, Thessalonica, Corinth, and a challenging intellectual dialogue between Paul and the philosophers of Athens on Mars Hill. The message of

Christianity, with its emphasis on the one true God and resurrected Savior, did not fit well in a culture of many gods and idols. However, several churches were planted by Paul in cities such as Corinth, Thessalonica, Colossae, and Ephesus, and the gospel grew in power and strength.

3.) *The Roman Empire* – The Roman Empire continued to be hostile to the message of Christianity, long after Rome crucified Christ under the direction of Pontius Pilate. Persecutions of the church under the Caesars such as Nero, Caligula, Domitian and others are well documented in history. The book of Revelation is virtually a commentary on the oppressive and hateful attitude of Rome toward Jesus Christ and the church. In spite of this, Paul was able to have influence for Christ in Rome, and Christianity in the fourth century under the influence of Constantine, became widely accepted and endorsed by the Roman Empire.

4.) *Pseudo-Christianity* – Pseudo-Christianity represented a form of Christianity rife with doctrinal and behavioral errors. These movements were far more insidious and dangerous to the Christian message than any of the aforementioned adversaries of Christ. Heresies in the form of *Legalism* (Galatians), *Gnosticism* (Colossians), and *Docetism* (Epistles of John) were all addressed by Paul and John in their epistles. There were elements of truth in these movements but enough heresy in them to pervert and alter the simple message of the grace of Christ. Paul, in particular, was continually calling the church to stay true to the Jesus Christ who died for them, providing a salvation of freedom, purity, and grace.

These four forces were powerfully intimidating opponents of Christianity with prestige, physical power, money, and influence in high places, all dimensions the early church lacked. Yet, in spite of these formidable challenges which came against them, defenders of the Christian faith in the first century and beyond were able to overcome these four influences, while greatly impacting the world with the message of Christ. Paul affirms the power of the gospel.

> *I am not ashamed of the gospel, because it is the power of God for the salvation of everyone who believes: first for the Jew, then for the Gentile.* Romans 1:16

Daniel, a sixth-century BC prophet, was given a glimpse of the coming power of Jesus when he interpreted the dream of Nebuchadnezzar in Daniel 2. The king dreamed of a human statue whose bodily components were composed of different precious metals. We know, by interpretation, that this statue symbolically represented four successive major political empires beginning with Babylon, ruled by Nebuchadnezzar himself. The king also was shown an everlasting kingdom and a stone coming from the heavens, smashing the statue to pieces and destroying it.

> *In the time of those kings, the God of heaven will set up a kingdom that will never be destroyed, nor will it be left to another people. It will crush all those kingdoms and bring them to an end, but it will itself endure forever. This is the meaning of the vision of the rock cut out of a mountain, but not by human hands—a rock that broke the iron, the bronze, the clay, the silver and the gold to pieces. "The great God*

> *has shown the king what will take place in the future. The dream is true and the interpretation is trustworthy."* Daniel 2:44-45

The stone, which obliterated the statue of nations, was none other than the kingdom of God which Christ introduced to the world when He came to earth. This is the same kingdom the church is advancing today. It is not a kingdom of human strength or effort manifested in physical weapons and armies. It is a kingdom from God that rules in the hearts of mankind, empowered by the Holy Spirit who lives inside of all true follower of Christ. Jesus passed this kingdom on to His church:

> *And I tell you that you are Peter, and on this rock I will build my church, and the gates of Hades will not overcome it. I will give you the keys of the kingdom of heaven; whatever you bind on earth will be bound in heaven, and whatever you loose on earth will be loosed in heaven.* Matthew 16:18-19

Jesus has given His church, based on His death and resurrection, the keys of authority to right what is wrong in our world and bring the rule of God to every heart who will embrace the Lord Jesus. It is to this end that we should declare the gospel of Christ to our culture with confidence, boldness, meekness and expectation. After all, this is what Jesus commanded His followers to do:

> *He said to them, "Go into all the world and preach the good news to all creation."* Mark 16:15

CHAPTER 3

WE PRESENT NOTHING BUT THE FACTS

Some would advance the notion that presenting unbelievers with facts and evidence supporting Christian claims is an exercise in futility which only appeals to the fallen nature of man. Since salvation is ultimately the work of the Holy Spirit, some would argue that any use of reason and logic is a waste of time and, ultimately, ineffectual in its intended result. Although, we should not ignore the efficacious work of the Holy Spirit in the process of salvation and that facts and persuasion alone will never usher a man in the kingdom of God, there is still value in approaching the skeptic on the basis of Christian evidence and facts. Challenging the skeptics while appealing to evidence is often advocated and practiced in Scripture. This is a valid approach to evangelism.

The Scriptures Exhort Us to Defend Our Faith

Christianity was birthed in history and lived out openly before a watching world. Because of this, the Christian faith invites investigation. Believers should not be afraid to openly encourage skeptics to ask questions and examine the claims of their faith. In fact, the Bible exhorts believers to be ready to answer these interrogations.

Peter admonishes us to defend our faith

Scripture is bold and clear about the importance of defending our faith before the skeptics:

> *But in your hearts set apart Christ as Lord. Always be prepared to give an answer to everyone who asks you to give the reason for the hope that you have. But do this with gentleness and respect.*
> 1 Peter 3:15-16

The Greek word for *answer* is *apologeia* from which we derive the word *apologetics*. It means simply *to defend.* Notice in this Scripture the balance between knowledge and sensitivity. Apologetics is not intended to be vicious and caustic. Our goal should never be to win arguments by hurting someone or flaunting off our knowledge in some conceited way. Our intent is to ultimately invite men and women to come to Jesus Christ, because we believe that He is the only true way to God. Our defense should be solely based on our compassion for the lost, not self-aggrandizement.

Paul was an excellent lawyer for the defense

The Apostle Paul defined his main role as defending (*apologeia*) the gospel to his culture. Notice his liberal use of the word defense:

> *Brothers and fathers, listen now to my defense.* Acts 22:1

> *It is right for me to feel this way about all of you, since I have you in my heart; for whether I am in chains or defending and confirming the gospel, all of you share in God's grace with me.* Philippians 1:7

> *The latter do so in love, knowing that I am put here for the defense of the gospel.* Philippians 1:16

Paul stood as a lawyer in the courtroom of the public square and presented a very convincing defense of the Christian faith. He was confident because he had the facts on his side. Many cults and religions do not invite investigation however, the Christian faith thrives on it. History is full of examples of skeptics who researched the claims of Christianity and were later converted (e.g., Frank Morrison, Sir William Ramsay, C. S. Lewis and Josh McDowell).

The Book of Acts: A Model on How to Defend Our Viewpoint

We live in a day where the cultural mantra is, "We just need to all get along." Somehow, in our multicultural, lets-not-offend-anybody society, we are taught it is wrong to debate, argue in a scholarly fashion, or attempt to persuade someone that our position on a given religious matter is the best one. We are often branded as "mean spirited" if we challenge the critic by arguing the uniqueness of our position. After all, we wouldn't want to hurt anyone's feelings. Our intent is not to argue from the standpoint of meanness. However, Scripture supports the idea of arguing and debating the case for Christianity openly in the public arena. In the book of Acts, we are treated to a number of instances where good debate and reason were employed to defend the credibility of Christianity before the world.

Paul reasoned at Thessalonica

Paul's second missionary journey took him to Thessalonica, an ancient city of Macedonia in Northern Greece, where he discovered a Jewish synagogue. He seized the opportunity to present the case for Christianity in a persuasive and intelligent fashion. Notice the scholarly words such as *reasoned*, *explaining*, and *proving* Luke used to describe Paul's actions:

> *As his custom was, Paul went into the synagogue, and on three Sabbath days he reasoned with them from the Scriptures, explaining and proving that the Christ had to suffer and rise from the dead. "This Jesus I am proclaiming to you is the Christ," he said. Some of the Jews were persuaded and joined Paul and Silas, as did a large number of God-fearing Greeks and not a few prominent women.* Acts 17:2-4

Paul didn't worry about offending people; he argued persuasively and won some converts by the power of God in the process.

Paul persuaded at Athens

Athens was the world-center of secular thinking in the days of Paul. The philosophers of Athens regularly discussed every prevailing philosophy known to the ancient world. One of the favorite gathering places of these erudite scholars was in the public marketplace or agora. Notice that Paul reasoned with individuals there when he arrived:

> *So he reasoned in the synagogue with the Jews and the God-fearing Greeks, as well as in the marketplace day by day with those who happened to be there.* Acts 17:17

Another popular place where these Athenian scholars gathered to debate the latest philosophy was Mars Hill or, in Greek, the Areopagus. The philosophers of Athens brought Paul to the Areopagus to listen to what he had to say. Paul gladly obliged.

> *Paul then stood up in the meeting of the Areopagus and said: "Men of Athens! I see that in every way you are very religious. For as I walked around and looked carefully at your objects of worship, I even found an altar with this inscription: TO AN UNKNOWN GOD. Now what you worship as something unknown I am going to proclaim to you."* Acts 17:22-23

These philosophers' erudition and reputation failed to intimidate Paul. He had the facts and reason on his side. In fact, Paul even gained converts as a result of his presentation.

> *A few men became followers of Paul and believed. Among them was Dionysius, a member of the Areopagus, also a woman named Damaris, and a number of others.* Acts 17:34

It is important to take notice that at this citadel of philosophy and religious thought, Paul did not hesitate to demonstrate the superiority of the Christian God and Savior. We will have much more to say about Paul's encounter on Mars Hill later.

Paul proved his case at Corinth

Corinth was renowned as a pagan and wicked city full of temples erected to idols. These temples contained numerous religious symbols. This city was also synonymous with sexual deviancy and other lewd behaviors. Through Paul's ministry, a church was established in Corinth and there was a letter from Paul addressed to them which bears their name. This was not a city for the timid Christian who didn't want to offend anyone. Again, in Corinth, we find Paul boldly and vigorously defending his Christian faith with cogent and persuasive arguments:

> *For he vigorously refuted the Jews in public debate, proving from the Scriptures that Jesus was the Christ.* Acts 18:28

Paul argued at Ephesus

Ephesus was the home of the temple of Diana as well as many other temples and shrines devoted to the numerous gods of Greece. Ephesus was a religious hub of the ancient world. Paul was not intimidated or shy about sharing his faith there. He reasoned persuasively in Ephesus:

> *Paul entered the synagogue and spoke boldly there for three months, arguing persuasively about the kingdom of God.* Acts 19:8

Three emphatic Greek words are used in these texts to represent arguing, persuading, or debating. Notice how prevalent they are in the book of Acts:

1. *dialogemia* - meaning *dispute, dialogue, discuss* - found in Acts 17:3, 17; 18:4, 19

2. *peithō* - meaning *persuade, prevail, win an argument* - found in Acts 13:45, 19:8, 17:4, 26:28, 2 Cor. 5:11

3. *paratithimī* - *set before as proof* and *open up to what is obvious* - found in Acts 17:3

Paul challenged King Agrippa

Paul was arrested on numerous occasions for sharing his faith and in several incidents was ushered before the authorities to defend his zealous activities on behalf of Christ. On one of those occasions, King Agrippa, the acting king of Judea, listened to Paul's defense of Christianity. The apostle rigorously appealed to the king's reason and logic in defending the resurrection of Christ. It is clear that Paul, concerning the resurrection, was presenting facts clearly known to those in the first century:

> *"...that the Christ would suffer and, as the first to rise from the dead, would proclaim light to his own people and to the Gentiles." At this point Festus interrupted Paul's defense. "You are out of your mind, Paul!" he shouted. "Your great learning is driving you insane." "I am not insane, most excellent Festus," Paul replied. "What I am saying is true and reasonable. The king is*

> *familiar with these things, and I can speak freely to him. I am convinced that none of this has escaped his notice, because it was not done in a corner."* Acts 26:23-26

Four observations stand out in Paul's defense of the resurrection of Christ before King Agrippa:

1. The resurrection of Christ was a fact.

2. The event transpired in the open, not in secret.

3. The king knew the facts and should have known better than to dismiss it.

4. The king made no attempt to refute Paul's claims.

Clearly the tenor of the book of Acts is that defenders of the Christian faith were bold and convincing in their proofs and presentations of the fundamentals of their faith. They were not cautious or timid. Maybe that is why the early church had such an incredible impact on the pagan world of the day.

Writers of Scripture Appealed to Facts and Reason

Contrary to contemporary views of Scripture that relegate the Bible to the genre of fantasy and myth, the Bible is very credible in its details and historical information. The authors of the Bible personally testify to the accuracy of their writings by appealing to facts and reason.

Luke appealed to scholarship

Luke, who authored both the gospel of Luke and the companion book of Acts, goes out of his way to assure the reader of his painstaking effort to present accurate information in his gospel. He was both a physician and a historian. By profession and temperament, Luke was accustomed to recording accuracy and detail. In the opening verse of his gospel, he makes it clear that his writings are the result of meticulous attention to detail and research:

> *Many have undertaken to draw up an account of the things that have been fulfilled among us, just as they were handed down to us by those who from the first were eyewitnesses and servants of the word. Therefore, since I myself have carefully investigated everything from the beginning, it seemed good also to me to write an orderly account for you, most excellent Theophilus, so that you may know the certainty of the things you have been taught.* Luke 1:1-4

Luke employs the Greek word *parakoluō* for the words translated *have carefully investigated everything*. This word means *to follow closely a course* or *plan of action*. He is expressing that he stayed on the trail of his research, like a dogged reporter following a good story. Luke had investigated everything carefully and did not drift off into fantasy or speculation.

In verse 4, two other very important words appear to emphasize the accuracy and reliability of Luke's writings. The word translated *know* is *epiginōskō*, meaning *full knowledge.* Luke intends to assure us that he is not hiding anything but revealing the full story as it pertains to Christ. The word rendered *certainty* is *asphaleia.* It is made up of *sphallō*, which means *to fall*, preceded by the Greek letter *alpha*, which negates the word, resulting in the translation *certainty*. The idea of security and safety is inherent in the word. In Acts 5:23, it is translated *securely*, and in 1 Thessalonians 5:3 rendered *safety*. Luke is declaring to his audience that his writing is accurate and reliable in every recorded detail, making it worthwhile and safe to read and embrace.

Paul resorted to the obvious

Many have asked the question, "Why hasn't God made Himself more known to the world?" The fact is that God has made His power and presence obvious to all who live on planet earth. Paul appeals to what is logical and reasonable when he condemns the world as without excuse when it comes to embracing the God of the Bible. Paul invites mankind to use rational and reasonable processes in considering the stars in the heavens as indicators of the existence of a powerful creator. Unfortunately, much of mankind is too obtuse to even understand even rudiment information readily available to them, just by observing the skies:

> *The wrath of God is being revealed from heaven against all the godlessness and wickedness of men who suppress the truth by their wickedness, since what may be known about God is plain to them, because God has made it plain to them. For since the creation of the world God's invisible qualities—his eternal power and divine nature—have been clearly seen, being understood from*

> *what has been made, so that men are without excuse.* Romans 1:18-20

The cornerstone of Paul's preaching was the resurrection of Christ from the dead. He did not appeal to fantasy, myth, or conjecture when it came to this unparalleled event. Instead, he resorted to evidence and fact. Paul was too intelligent to make a statement about Christ's being seen by many after His resurrection if, in fact, it had not happened. Notice how Paul appeals to evidence:

> *For what I received I passed on to you what was most important and what had also been passed on to me—that Christ died for our sins, just as the Scriptures said. He was buried, and he was raised from the dead on the third day, as the Scriptures said. He was seen by Peter and then by the twelve apostles. After that, he was seen by more than five hundred of his followers at one time, most of whom are still alive, though some have died by now. Then he was seen by James and later by all the apostles. Last of all, I saw him, too, long after the others, as though I had been born at the wrong time.* 1 Corinthians 15:3-5

In this passage, Paul used six lines of defense in his argument defending the resurrection of Christ. Let's look at them one by one.

1. *Peter* - The Bible records the mention of Jesus' initial post-resurrection appearance to Peter in Luke 24:34. Also, we know from Galatians 1:18 that Paul spent time with Peter for about two weeks

in Jerusalem long after his conversion. Peter could have easily conveyed this information to Paul.

2. *The Twelve* - Luke 24:36-42 and John 20:19-20 records Jesus' appearance to the original disciples after His resurrection. It was to them that He went out of His way to demonstrate He was physically raised from the dead by inviting them to touch his wounds and also by dining with them.

3. *More than 500* - There is not a specific recording of Jesus' appearance to the five hundred, but apparently Paul had a measure of familiarity with them because he knew that some were still alive, who could testify to the resurrection.

4. *James* - James was Jesus's younger brother. We know that the Lord's siblings were skeptical of identifying Jesus as the Messiah and were reluctant to embrace Him in any fashion (Mark 3:21, 31-35; John 7:1-10). Then, James appears in the upper room in Acts 1:14 and is later referenced in Acts 12:17. In Galatians 1:19, Paul speaks of visiting James, who was a leader in the Jerusalem church. There is no question that James became an ardent follower of his half-brother. This is why Jesus would have appeared to him.

5. *All the apostles* - This is obviously a reference to a larger group of apostles outside of the original twelve. This group could have easily been those included in the upper room in Acts 1:21-22. Paul would have been able to have personal contact with many of them.

6. *Paul* - The last line of defense comes from the life of Paul himself. The conversion of Paul is the most dramatic and unlikely spiritual transformation in the history of Christianity. Someone, with so much animas and vitriol toward Jesus Christ and His followers, to so fervently become a disciple of Christ and propagator of the faith, would require some dramatic and defining event to bring it about. We know that Paul received this life changing appearance from Christ on the Damascus road, recorded in Acts 9:1-9, and recounted two more times in the book of Acts.

Peter persuaded with facts

Peter could have relied on reputation and guile to make his defense of Jesus. But he made it clear that his preaching and writing about the Savior were based on fact, eyewitnesses, and miraculous events Jesus performed which were observed. Peter affirmed in many situations that what he taught and believed was clearly empirical, credible, and verifiable:

His preaching at Pentecost

> *Men of Israel, listen to this: Jesus of Nazareth was a man accredited by God to you by miracles, wonders and signs, which God did among you through him, as you yourselves know. This man was handed over to you by God's set purpose and foreknowledge; and you, with the help of wicked men, put him to death by nailing him to the cross. But God raised him from the dead,*

> *freeing him from the agony of death, because it was impossible for death to keep its hold on him.* Acts 2:22-24

In these verses, Peter boldly declares that Jesus of Nazareth was accredited by God. The word translated *accredited* is *apodeiknumi*. It is in the perfect tense, which emphasizes the continuous result that Jesus was accredited by God. This is an interesting word meaning *to set forth, point out, prove*, or *proclaim*. It is used in Acts 25:7 in the sense that Paul's accusers could not prove their charges against him. This is a word about credentials and verification. The astonishing miracles Jesus performed throughout His ministry and His resurrection from the dead, provided tangible credentials to support His claims that He was God and the Messiah of Israel.

His encounter with Cornelius

> *We are witnesses of everything he did in the country of the Jews and in Jerusalem. They killed him by hanging him on a tree, but God raised him from the dead on the third day and caused him to be seen. He was not seen by all the people, but by witnesses whom God had already chosen—by us who ate and drank with him after he rose from the dead. He commanded us to preach to the people and to testify that he is the one whom God appointed as judge of the living and the dead.* Acts 10:39-42

In Peter's conversation with Cornelius, he appeals to his personal eyewitness of everything Jesus did, as well as those who witnessed His resurrection. The translation *had already chosen* comes from *procheirotoneō*, which literally means *to stretch out the hand before to give a vote.* The root word of *procheirotoneō* is *cheirotoneō* which is used in Acts 14:23 and 2 Corinthians 8:19, where it is translated *appointed* and *chosen*, respectively. This demonstrates God's sovereignty even in choosing the witnesses of the resurrection. The details surrounding Christ's death and resurrection were carefully orchestrated by God so that the reality of the events would be beyond dispute. Every detail regarding the resurrection of Christ was perfectly set in place by God. If God could give such attention to detail concerning the events of His Son, He can also do this for us.

His writings

> *We did not follow cleverly invented stories when we told you about the power and coming of our Lord Jesus Christ, but we were eyewitnesses of his majesty.* 2 Peter 1:16

Few passages express the reliability and authenticity of Scripture better than this one. Peter, who was a primary source for the recordings of the life of Christ, goes out of his way to debunk the notion that the Scriptures, particularly the ones he penned, were full of unreliable myths and hearsay.

The translation *cleverly invented* is from the Greek word *sophizō*, which means *to give wisdom.* This word is used in a positive sense concerning the Scriptures in 2 Timothy 3:15. The idea here is *to reason out* or *cleverly contrive with human wisdom and sophistry*. The point is that the Scriptures did not originate with human wisdom

The translation *stories* is derived from *muthos*, which transliterates into our English word *myth*. It is translated *myth* in 1Timothy 1:4, 4:7; 2 Timothy 4:4, and Titus 1:14. This word often stood for mythical stories about the gods. It represented tales that were fables and essentially false. When put together, these words represent cleverly thought out and contrived fiction. Peter emphatically denies that this is the case with the Word of God. The Bible is truth, not fiction.

Conversely, Peter offers support for the veracity and reliability of the Word of God. The translation *eyewitnesses* is from *epoptēs*, which means *to see* or *behold with the eye*. The verb form, *epopteuō*, is used in 1 Peter 2:12 and 3:2, where it is translated *see*. A word similar to *epoptēs*, *autoptēs*, is used in Luke 1:2 where it is also rendered *eyewitnesses.* Peter was an eyewitness of all that happened to Jesus. Eyewitnesses are considered primary evidence in support of any claim, and are essential for historical authentication. The Scriptures do not rest upon made-up stories, but on reliable eyewitness accounts.

John used empirical terms

John appealed to his own personal relationship with the Lord Jesus when defending who Christ was. Notice John's use of empirical terms to corroborate the credibility of his writings concerning Jesus:

> *That which was from the beginning, which we have heard, which we have seen with our eyes,*

which we have looked at and our hands have touched—this we proclaim concerning the Word of life. The life appeared; we have seen it and testify to it, and we proclaim to you the eternal life, which was with the Father and has appeared to us. We proclaim to you what we have seen and heard, so that you also may have fellowship with us. And our fellowship is with the Father and with his Son, Jesus Christ. 1 John 1:1-3

When John writes of his having *heard*, *seen* and *touched* Jesus, he employs the Greek perfect tense in his descriptions. This perfect tense emphasizes something which has happened in the past with ongoing effects of the experience. John's usage of this tense conveys the idea that his experience with Jesus was as real at the time of his writing as it was when he first walked with the Lord. John is assuring us that his depictions of Christ were not the result of hallucinations or fantasies but based on tangible and palpable evidence from a primary source.

Jesus Appealed to Evidence

Many skeptics of Christianity maintain the notion that Jesus walked around on a cloud like some mystery cult leader. However, when one of His disciples was in the throes of severe doubt, Jesus did not ask him to blindly follow Him in an irrational leap of faith. He appealed to Thomas with facts:

Then he said to Thomas, "Put your finger here; see my hands. Reach out your hand and put it into my side. Stop doubting and believe." John 20:27

> *"Look at my hands and my feet. It is I myself! Touch me and see; a ghost does not have flesh and bones, as you see I have."* Luke 24:39

Jesus invited Thomas to employ his senses of sight and touch to verify that Jesus was truly risen. Our Lord evens mentions His flesh and bones, which dispelled the notion He was a ghost. A word of caution is in order here. We must be careful not to become fact-producing machines thinking that we must always come up with a nifty explanation to lead someone to Christ. Jesus, after the Thomas incident, stated that many would come to follow Him without having to receive tangible proof of seeing Jesus. Faith is a matter of the heart and many will reject Christ in the face of overwhelming evidence. However, there are times when it is appropriate to challenge the skeptic by presenting evidence to him. Thomas needed this tangible demonstration of the Lord's resurrection to assuage his honest doubt and understandable skepticism. Sometimes this may be what the Holy Spirit uses to convict a man's heart concerning the reality of Jesus Christ.

CHAPTER 4
DEFINING KEY TERMS

Words like *faith*, *proof*, *truth*, *miracles*, and *history* are essential terms when it comes to discussing the credibility of Christianity. However, the non-Christian often views these concepts differently than people of faith. When a Christian says that he believes in God, his idea of "God" may have a totally different meaning in the mind of a non-Christian, as well as the nature of belief. Modern culture often approaches truth differently as well. Many non-believers equate the Christian faith with gullibility, stupidity, and blind credulity. A good example is the theory of evolution, also known as Classic Darwinism. Many supporting principles exist for the biblical view of creation and there are tremendous gaps and unanswered questions in the theory of evolution. Yet, to espouse creationism in our culture places us in the category of the unlearned and exposes us to ridicule and derision. As apologists, it is important to always remember that our goal is to help the non-Christian consider Christianity, as he would any other area of life. Everyone lives by faith. Each person has a way of verifying what is true and what is not, while believing in things he has never seen. This section will help explain the nature of proof, faith, miracles, truth and history so that we can relate better to the secular person.

The Nature of Faith

Many associate the term *faith* with fantasy and irrationality. It is important that we address this erroneous perception. As we have stated: all human beings live by faith in some way or another. Let's examine some key elements that define the nature of biblical faith.

A true conviction, not a blind leap in the dark

Some would argue that spiritual faith is a blind leap in the dark or something to be embraced because it makes us feel good, not because it is true or verifiable. They would argue that solid reasons or a factual basis are not essential for having a religious faith. The Bible disagrees with this approach.

> *Now faith is being sure of what we hope for and certain of what we do not see.* Hebrews 11:1

According to Hebrews 11:1, faith is a conviction based on a solid foundation. This verse expresses the idea that faith is predicated on what we are certain about. The Greek word for *certain* is *elenkō,* and it conveys the idea of a *deep conviction.* It is important that as Christians, we know what we believe as well as why. Many followers of Christ lack confidence because they are living off someone else's convictions. True faith is based on a solid conviction that what and who we are embracing is real and sure. There is solid reasoning and evidence to back up and support our faith.

Based on fact, not fiction

Normally, we don't associate faith and fact as related subjects. Faith often is relegated to the invisible, irrational and emotional, while facts encompass the arena we can see with our physical eyes. However, most of us believe in something because there is good reason for it. Very seldom do we embrace or place faith in anything that has not been researched or tested. For instance, we eat certain foods because there is reason to believe they will help us and not hurt us. We trust or place faith in people because of sound observational conclusions regarding their character. We exercise faith in many ways because of good factual analysis. Our text in Hebrews says that faith is what we are *sure* about:

> *Now faith is being sure of what we hope for....* Hebrews 11:1

The word translated *sure* is *hupostasis* and it literally means *substance, support base,* or *a foundation.* Hebrews 1:3 translates this word *being* in reference to the nature and essence of Christ. Faith is concrete, factual, and substantial. In another place, Luke encourages faith based on sound research and investigation:

> *Therefore, since I myself have carefully investigated everything from the beginning, it seemed good also to me to write an orderly account for you, most excellent Theophilus.* Luke 1:3

Again, let us approach the non-Christian in a way that he can understand. Every day he lives by faith. He trusts things and commits himself to ideas and processes because there is evidence that these things work. He is willing to sit on a chair because he knows something about what it is made of and experience tells him that it can hold his body. Christianity should be no less believable.

Corresponds with reality

If the Christian faith is real, it should make sense and correspond with reality. When Paul confronted King Agrippa and said that the resurrection did not occur in secret but was fully known to the king, Paul was appealing to common sense and reason. The king did not deny what Paul said or make some feeble attempt to explain the apostle's words away. King Agrippa knew the truth and credibility of Paul's words.

> *The king is familiar with these things, and I can speak freely to him. I am convinced that none of this has escaped his notice, because it was not done in a corner.* Acts 26:26

This principle also applies to a belief in God. Acknowledging the existence of a Creator logically makes sense and corresponds with our sense of reality. The secular mind, by removing God, has postulated a world without Him to be more reasonable than a world with Him. Yet, not to believe in a Supreme Being leaves our understanding of life with major gaps and numerous unanswered questions. It is more feasible to believe in a Creator. C. S. Lewis poignantly address this with this statement, "An egg which came from no bird is no more natural than a bird which had existed from all eternity." (C. S. Lewis. *God in the Dock,* p. 211) The Bible declares how foolish it is not to embrace the living God and classifies those who deny His existence, or who act in a way that He in reality does not matter, as fools:

> *The fool says in his heart, "There is no God." They are corrupt, and their ways are vile; there is no one who does good.* Psalm 53:1

> *For although they knew God, they neither glorified him as God nor gave thanks to him, but their thinking became futile and their foolish hearts were darkened. Although they claimed to be wise, they became fools.* Romans 1:21-22

Do not confuse the supernatural with fantasy. The supernatural is a real world that has been observed throughout history. Fantasy is a make-believe world with little connection to our experience. The Bible was written in a real world, not a fantasy world. Faith is not a blind leap into fantasy; it is a belief in a factual, verifiable world. It makes far more sense to believe in a God of creation and order than to relegate the world's existence to chance and random processes.

The Elusiveness of Proof

Often in our discourse with the non-believer, the Christian will be faced with the daunting challenge of proving everything he believes: from the existence of God to the resurrection of Christ. This can be an intimidating and frustrating exercise. When it comes to proving something, there are some key principles we must understand.

Sorry: we cannot prove what we believe

Be careful of the trap. This request to prove conclusively the authenticity of our beliefs is impossible to fulfill, since proof is determined through observation and scientific analysis. It is difficult to prove anything one cannot see or something which happened hundreds of years ago beyond our grasp of recognition. The non-Christian should be confronted with the fact that he also believes in things he has never seen and cannot prove. We do not empirically see love, faith, or hope. How can we prove that we loved a deceased relative, or that we were happy when we were six year old? Is it possible, to prove beyond the shadow of a doubt what we had for dinner three months ago? Can I prove the emotions I felt when I saw the magnificent scenery at a national park? Has anyone seen the wind so they can tell you what it looks like? We believe that the wind exists because we have observed the evidence of what it does, not because we see it as a corporeal substance. We often accept the experiences of others, the testimony of intriguing people, and the scholarly wisdom of historians without ever empirically witnessing what they were writing or talking about. Most people believe that Julius Caesar historically existed but none of us has directly seen him. Just because we cannot empirically prove something exists, does not necessarily discredit its validity or reality.

In the movie, *Contact*, an agnostic scientist named Dr. Eleanor Arroway (played by Jodie Foster) maintains a position questioning whether God exists, a fact which she dogmatically proclaims cannot be proven. However, at the end of the movie, Dr. Arroway is caught in her own "proof" trap as she has an experience on her space journey she cannot prove to her doubters because the instruments monitoring the events failed to record what she saw or experienced. Only static was recorded. A congressional committee evaluating her journey, comes to the conclusion that what she experienced was possibly a hoax designed by the deceased creator of the machine in which she travelled. The irony of this is, although she cannot prove her experience happened, Arroway asks the skeptical committee to accept the truth of her testimony on "faith", an exercise previously she would not afford to God's existence. She learns a valuable lesson that some things can exist even though they cannot be tangibly proven.

The non-Christian, as well as the Christian, espouses many things they cannot empirically prove. Both groups live in a world of faith. The real question is which worldview or belief system is the more believable. If the non-Christian wants proof from us, he has to realize that he cannot offer proof for his own beliefs either. The evolutionist, if he is honest, must admit that his postulations are theories, just as the Christian should acknowledge that his viewpoint is a theory as well. Both viewpoints operate in the realm of the theoretical; the question is which is the most probable and reasonable? We believe that when the evidence is in, one has to defy logic and sound reason not to recognize the viability and accuracy of the Christian faith.

We live in a world of probabilities not certainties

Let's face it, when it comes to proof, it is important to realize that, more often than not, we live in a world of probabilities and not proofs. When we consider the existence of God, the reliability of the Bible, the resurrection of Christ, or the miraculous, we can only offer information which suggests a high probability that these events occurred and are true. As an example, I cannot prove that the Bible is the Word of God but I can demonstrate, through various means, there is a high probably it is a supernatural book written from the mind of God.

The same is true for the resurrection of Christ. We cannot prove, beyond the shadow of doubt, this spectacular event historically occurred but, through the historical process of verification, it is possible to educe a compelling argument that there is a high degree of probability it did. Again, this is the way most people evaluate things in their lives. As an illustration, I might ask someone what he or she had for breakfast three weeks ago. If they told me cereal but could not empirically prove beyond a doubt that what they said is what they really ate, would I totally disregard their statements as false? The answer is "no". Based on their integrity, honesty, and consistency of telling the truth observed over a period of time, I would logically conclude there is a high probability that what they told me was the truth. The same applies to spiritual ideas as well.

The Truth about Truth

Christianity is a religion based on verifiable truths. We invite the skeptic to recognize that there is a foundation of truth and fact underlying all Christian experiences and claims. This automatically puts us at odds with our very relativistic society where many deny the existence of absolute truths. The whole idea of what is true has become muddy and murky. Ideas, values and morals, once deemed immutable, now change with the ebb and flow of human opinion. Christians are uncomfortable with this approach to life, since we are guided by absolute truths and affirm that our Christian faith is based on them. Therefore, it is important to understand certain principles when it comes to Christianity and truth.

Truth is foundational to Christianity

While the Christian faith is based on absolutes, our culture wants everything to be flexible and negotiable. Jesus said that His life was about the truth. Pilate responded by asking Jesus what truth really was. Jesus responded:

> *"You are a king, then!" said Pilate. Jesus answered, "You are right in saying I am a king. In fact, for this reason I was born, and for this I came into the world, to testify to the truth. Everyone on the side of truth listens to me." "What is truth?" Pilate asked. With this he went out again to the Jews and said, "I find no basis for a charge against him."* John 18:37-38

Jesus equated His person and character with truth. He is the measurement by which all truth is determined. In another passage, Jesus affirmed that to know and follow Him is to know and follow truth. In Jesus' words, truth is absolute, and truth can be known:

> *Jesus answered, "I am the way and the truth and the life. No one comes to the Father except through me."* John 14:6

By declaring that He is the standard by which truth is measured, He is also implying that anything or anyone contradicting Him violates the truth. The Roman Caesars could claim all day long that they were gods to be worshipped, yet the Christian faith would recognize this as untrue.

Truth can be tested by standards

Most of us desire to know right from wrong and what is true from what is not. In a day when we are told that everything is relative and there are no absolute truths (which contradicts the previous statement) the world longs to hear the voice of truth. We raise the question, "Do all religions possess the truth?" Our answer is, "No!" They may possess truth in some areas but, where they disagree with Christ and the Word of God, their tenets cannot be true. For instance, if a religion, as part of their core tenet of beliefs, espouses the view that mankind can earn his way to heaven through a series of human works and efforts, this would be deemed by the Christian as untrue because the Bible declares unequivocally that salvation cannot be earned by human effort (Ephesians 2:8-9). Many people believe that it doesn't matter which religion one belongs to, as long as it makes them feel good or causes some positive change in their life. However, the fact is that all religions cannot be true when they claim conflicting views not taught in the Bible about life, heaven, and spiritual destiny. Therefore, it is important that we study what truth is and what it is not.

The quest for determining whether something is true or not can be determined by some very important principles and processes. Norman Geisler, in his great work, *Christian Apologetics*, and Ravi Zecharias, in his classic book, *Can Man Live Without God,* help us understand the basis for evaluating what is true and what is not true.

They suggest that truth must meet five tests. These tests apply to anyone seeking to know whether something is true or not.

1. *Is it logically consistent?* For instance, if I say that I drew some square circles, you would know that this is not true. A degree of logic determines truth. This ties in with the nature of faith as well. Christian beliefs and doctrine are very logical, which forms the basis of faith.

2. *Is it empirically adequate?* Can it be tested? If I came to someone and stated that I had seen an elephant in the parking lot and there was no way to test this statement, one would have every right to disbelieve me. To determine what is true, it must be possible to analyze and test any statement objectively. When we speak of the Christian faith, we are speaking of something that can be verified and tested, particularly through the disciplines of archaeology, textual criticism, and verification of documents. The Christian faith is not a mystical pipe dream that exists in a vacuum.

3. *Is it experientially relevant?* Can I relate to what is being said? Does it have meaning in my life? Is it consistent with other things that I have experienced? For instance, we experience the rising of the sun every morning. If someone were to tell us that the sun had not come up today, based on our experience, we would have reason to doubt the truth of the assertion. This is important, especially as it pertains to our discussion regarding the "existence of God". God's existence is evident to most

people on planet earth which has an experiential component to it. Our experience tells us, based on everything we have observed and witnessed, that our planet had to have a creator to exist.

4. *Is it undeniable?* This test asks the question, "Is the statement or idea obvious and clear?" For instance, my existence is undeniable. If I can deny my existence, it means I exist, since I am stating the fact. If I cannot deny my existence, I exist. We know that a triangle must have three sides. If a shape has three sides, it is automatically a triangle. The truth is undeniable.

5. *Is it unaffirmable?* This point deals with statements that are obviously untrue. Just because something can be stated or educed does not make it true. We can say lots of things but they are not all true. For instance, if I said, "I cannot write in English," one would know that this is untrue because I am writing this book in English right now. The statement, "There are no such things as absolutes", is false because the statement itself is expressed in absolute terms. Geisler applies this principle of unaffirmability in refuting pantheism:

    The most fundamental criticism of a strictly pantheistic world view is that it is actually unaffirmable by man, for no finite individual really exists as an entity really different from God or the absolute. In essence a strict pantheist must affirm, "God is but I am not." But this is self-defeating, since one must exist in order to affirm that he does not exist. (Norman Geisler, *Christian Apologetics*, p. 187)

For Christianity to be true, it has to meet these five tests, and it does.

Truth is exclusive

If something is true, it cannot be untrue at the same time. That is why all religions are exclusive in their claims to represent the truth. For instance, if Jesus said that He is the only way to God and Hinduism teaches something opposite, both cannot be true. If Christian theology states that man is inherently sinful, while another religion declares that man is inherently good, we have a contradiction. If pantheistic religious views of the world maintain that the essence of their gods, human conscious and identity, and the material universe are one and indistinguishable from each other, while Christianity expresses the idea that God is separate from His creation, then we have two incompatible views which cannot be reconciled and true at the same time. The issue is to determine which religions are consistent with the five standards and tests stated above. Jesus Christ met all of these conditions for truth in His life. Affirm Him and we affirm truth. Ravi Zecharias sums it up well:

> *The issue, then, is not whether the belief system you espouse—monotheistic, atheistic, pantheistic, or otherwise—is exclusive. The issue is whether the answers to the four basic questions of life pertaining to origin, meaning, morality, and destiny within the context of each of these worldviews meets the test of truth. Are they logically consistent, are they empirically adequate, and are they experientially relevant? Do they meet the tests of unaffirmability and undeniability? The answers*

> *to life's four questions must in each instance correspond in reality, and the sum of the answers must cohere as a system.* (Ravi Zecharias. *Can Man Live Without God?* p. 126)

The Importance of Miracles

The Christian faith and the supernatural are inextricably woven together to form a story that has transpired over centuries. Since Christianity is rooted in the belief there is a God Who intervenes in the working of nature and in the lives of humanity, it is easy for people of religious persuasion to believe in miracles. In a secular culture that is increasingly prone to accept only what secular science advocates and believes, it is important that we open up a dialogue on the miraculous. The resurrection of Christ from the dead is the greatest miracle in which the Christian believes. It is vital to understand what we mean by *miracle* and why it is important to our faith. A good working definition of miracle is: *an extraordinary, visible act of divine power which is not normally seen in the everyday course of events.* Several aspects of miracles must be clarified since we have been conditioned by our secular culture to accept the idea that miracles cannot happen today.

Miracles are not anti-natural but supernatural

Those who believe in the supernatural and the miraculous are not anti-natural. We espouse that nature is good and wonderful. We know that God has placed marvelous things on the earth for us to enjoy. For instance, we may believe in the supernatural, miraculous power of God to heal, but we also accept that there are sound natural remedies for healing as well. The Christian does not advocate that the natural and supernatural are mutually exclusive, but co-exist together to form a balanced view of the universe. David Hume, the famous Scottish philosopher, concluded that miracles cannot occur because the laws of nature militate against the possibility of them happening. In other words, nature is always right and has the final say. In Hume's view, since miracles cannot occur, any suggestion that they have must defer to the laws of nature which rules against them happening. This circular line of reasoning by Hume eliminated any objective possibility or assessment of miracles since, by his definition, they could not happen in the first place. According to his analysis, the resurrection of Jesus Christ was an impossibility; the product of deception and false information, since natural thinking would automatically render the judgment that once an individual died, this type of event could not occur. Hume essentially eliminated the possibility of any objective analysis of miracles through this line of reasoning, regardless of the compelling evidence of history and research.

Miracles are not contradictory to nature

Miracles belong to the realm of the supernatural. Miracles do not contradict nature but merely expand our way of looking at nature. We simply believe that the natural and the supernatural co-exist as forces in our world. The way we perceive creation is often referred to as a worldview. A worldview is a grid through which we understand how and why the world functions as it does. To formulate his worldview, the Christian embraces a natural world and also a supernatural world. For instance, we believe that sickness can be derived from natural sources such as germs, genetics, and lack of a good diet and exercise. We also believe that sickness and disease could possibly originate from the demonic and invisible world. Both can be true and real. Jesus, during His ministry, did not violate nature or natural processes. He ate, drank, slept, made use of fire and traversed the Sea of Galilee in boats. He did indeed occasionally operate in the supernatural like when He turned water into wine at the wedding in Cana. However, when drinking wine on other occasions, we can assume the wine He drank originated from grapes that went through the natural process of growth and fermentation.

Miracles are not illogical in a world controlled by God

Believing in miracles doesn't indicate a lack of intelligence or common sense. In a world where God exists, it is very logical and reasonable to believe in miracles. It is only to the closed mind, which leaves no room for God in its worldview, that miracles seem illogical and impossible. Thomas, of doubting-Thomas fame, was skeptical that the miracle of Christ's resurrection had taken place. When Jesus showed him His scars from the cross, Thomas changed his mind.

Miracles are God's special operations

Natural events are God's *general* operations, while miracles represent His *special* manifestations. They are unique and dramatic in their impact and results. Miracles arrest attention and cause men to stand in awe of what they have seen. This is why, in the New Testament, words such as *fear*, *amazement*, *signs* and *wonders* are often associated with miracles. Sometimes religious folk mitigate the meaning and impact of miracles by loosely throwing around the term *miracle* to include common occurrences. Miracles are special and astounding, not ordinary. They are rare, not common, in their manifestations.

Miracles should not be explained in scientific terms

Miracles override and supersede natural explanations. Miracles cannot be quantified or explained by the "scientific method". Miracles belong to the realm of God and the supernatural. Therefore, they are best explained by religion, not science. Religion and science should be very compatible and work together for the good of society. There have been times in history where religion got in the way of true science, as in the case of Galileo who claimed that the sun, not the earth, stood in the center of the universe (Copernician view). This view incurred the wrath of the Catholic Church and they forced him to recant of his theory. Later, Galileo's hypothesis was proven to be scientifically true. We are now living in a time where science is attempting to usurp the role of religion in society by almost becoming a religion unto itself. We should seek balance and desire that religion and science not step on each other by becoming dogmatic on things they were never intended to oversee. This is especially relevant in the area of miracles.

Miracles should be investigated like other historical events

Since miracles are a part of history, they should be investigated in the same way that other historical events are researched. One should not dismiss, as David Hume did, the resurrection of Christ from the dead on the basis that miracles cannot happen, when adequate research and scholarship has not been applied to the subject. The resurrection of Christ from the dead should be evaluated on its merits like any other occurrence of history. The witness of those who observed and wrote about the events surrounding Christ's life, should be given serious consideration as primary sources of information as diligent investigative principles are applied. Also, those sources outside of the realm of Christianity should also be included in the verification process. When done so, the resurrection of Christ will be found to have great historical credibility.

Miracles remind us that there is another world beyond the physical

Miracles remind us there is more to our universe than what we see in the physical realm. They challenge us to recognize and seek a higher world, as real as the world we observe. According to Scripture, man was created in the image of God. Therefore, it is important for mankind to have a connection with the author of miracles: God Himself.

Miracles validated the ministry of Jesus

Jesus Christ's ministry and life were attested to by miracles of the highest degree. From His first miracle of turning the water into wine in John 2, to His greatest miracle in John 11 of raising Lazarus from the dead, miracles played a prominent role in supporting His claim that He was indeed the Son of God and the Messiah the Old Testament foretold. It was through His miracles that Jesus authenticated the fact that He came from heaven. John specifically explains that he recorded the miracles of Jesus to further authenticate His credentials as the Son of God:

> *Jesus did many other miraculous signs in the presence of his disciples, which are not recorded in this book. But these are written that you may believe that Jesus is the Christ, the Son of God, and that by believing you may have life in his name.* John 20:30-31

One cannot, with any degree of accuracy or credibility, separate Jesus Christ from His miracles and awesome displays of power authority. They are inextricably linked together and deserved to be evaluated and historically analyzed like any other event.

Christianity is History

History and Christianity must not and should not be divorced from each other. The biblical narrative was chronicled over thousands of years, while incorporating into its pages many civilizations, empires, kings, countries, coins, cities, rivers, mountains, people groups, and other aspects of the historical world. History, like truth and faith, is vitally linked to Christianity. If the historical facts surrounding the Christian narrative be proven false and unreliable, then one would have every right to question the validity of the spiritual aspects as well. Therefore, the history of Christianity should not be examined or analyzed any differently than secular history. Christians believe in a book which they claim is the Word of God. However, the Bible is far more than a book of spiritual truths and poignant aphorisms; it is also a record of ancient events. Jesus died on the cross, but that crucifixion took place in a certain location, at a particular time, carried out by many participants, by means of a well-known method of execution. The Bible was not written in an ivory tower or in a vacuum but was chronicled in the real world of conflict, war, and struggle. There are many resources available today for one to analyze historical events of the first century. R. K. Harrison has aptly stated:

> *Modern historians are not so heavily dependent on subjective literary sources as before, because the sciences of linguistics, sociology, anthropology, numismatics, and archaeology have become so developed.* (R.K. Harrison, *Introduction to the Old Testament* p.292.)

The Christian makes a mistake in not inviting the skeptic to examine the historical accuracy of the biblical record and the events it records. We should encourage critics to evaluate Christian history objectively, as they would any other historical person or event. There are some important principles to heed when analyzing biblical history.

Christian history should be approached objectively

There is a double standard in our world when it comes to history. Many approach secular history in one way and Christian history in another. They would have no problem accepting the historical identity and achievements of Julius Caesar or Alexander the Great, yet rankle sometimes at the thought that Jesus was indeed the historical figure recorded in the Bible. Remember, our goal as apologists is to invite the non-believer to evaluate and examine Christianity as he would other areas of his life. If one believes that Napoleon existed and executed events in history without having seen him, then it is also possible to believe that Jesus Christ existed as well, and performed the miracles recorded in the Bible.

It is vitally important to evaluate secular history and Christian history in the same way. History must be allowed to speak for itself. For instance, like David Hume, if we assume that miracles can't happen, we will never be historically objective about the resurrection of Christ because we have already ruled out the possibility that miracles can occur. Drawing conclusions based on unproved assumptions is referred to as the logical fallacy of "begging the question". However, if we analyze history objectively, we may find that historical miracles can still occur. Apologetics challenges the critic to submit the Christian faith to historical analysis, fully confident that the Bible can meet the test of such scrutiny. We ask the unbeliever to verify first, then believe.

Christian history should be analyzed in a scholarly manner

Historians use primary and secondary source material to verify the historical accuracy of their research. We learn from the past by trusting the writings of others who witnessed the individuals and events they wrote about. It is also important to examine the credibility of sources we use in our research. The events of Christianity are not only attested to by the biblical writers but also by Church Fathers, Roman and Jewish historians, and others who lived in the first century. We believe that George Washington lived because of associates and friends who attested to his life, and documents which bear his name, not because we have physically seen him. Therefore, sources in substantiating historical occurrences must be reliable and accurate. We should reject the arguments from critics of Christianity who have never taken the time to research the historical facts or even attempted to analyze the writings of the men closest to Jesus who chronicled the events of His life. This is intellectual dishonesty. When someone challenges our faith, it is imperative to ask them to provide support for their attacks and criticisms. Then we must be ready to defend our faith based on our own research.

Christianity should not be divorced from history. Yes, Christianity is spiritual but is also rooted in actual events that transpired before individuals who witnessed what occurred. What we preach and teach can only be true if history supports what we say. It is just as important and vital that records of cities, civilizations, kings, and events recorded in the Bible be as accurate and reliable as the spiritual aspects discussed.

ORIGIN
Meaning
Morality
Destiny

CHAPTER 5

ALL RELIGIONS ARE NOT EQUAL

As discussed in chapter 1, Christianity is unique in many ways. The Christian faith is based on a particular theology (study of God) and view of the world. When we defend Christianity to our society, we are defending some very special beliefs and principles woven into a narrative that explains the way life developed and now exists. There are some important things to keep in mind when defending Christian theology to the modern world.

Christian Theology: A Distinctive Set of Beliefs

Christian theology is based on a logical, well-designed set of beliefs and principles. One fact leads logically to another. We start with God and end with us. Christian theology can simply be defined this way:

- A force we call God, is eternal, not caused by anyone or anything, and is the Creator of the universe and man. Creation and mankind were perfect until human beings rebelled and allowed sin to enter the world and bring it to ruin, while also giving Satan a measure of authority and power over it.

- This Creator God, Who has a name and many attributes, has involved Himself with mankind throughout history and His activities have been recorded in historical documents known as the Holy Scripture. He also visited our world through the person of Jesus Christ. God's activities with man and His visitation to this earth through Jesus Christ, have been verified through primary and secondary documents that have been found to be reliable and accurate. Thus, the events recorded are true and trustworthy.

- Jesus Christ was born of a virgin via a miraculous conception. He was both God and man and lived among humanity demonstrating what the kingdom of God was like. His claim to deity was corroborated by fulfilling all Old-Testament prophecies about the Messiah (given hundreds of years before his birth), by living a miraculous life, and rising bodily from the dead. Therefore, He is God.

- Since Jesus, through His life, gave credence to Who He said He was, and did what He said He would do in rising from the dead, He has credentials enabling Him to claim authority over any other religion or religious personality and leader, as well as the right to demand worship and unbridled loyalty from His followers.

- Because of the superior credentials of Christ, His claims and discussions are valid and true. All other teachings from all other religious leaders must defer to Jesus Christ. Thus, His instructions about life, truth, sin, salvation, judgment, eternity and faith provide the comprehensive answer for all of man's problems. When Jesus said He was the only way to God, He was correct.

- It is incumbent upon mankind to personally embrace and believe in the God-Man-Savior for the forgiveness of sin, eternal redemption and a relationship with Almighty God. One's future and eternal destiny depends on it.

Christianity is Different from All Other Religions

One of the questions Christians are often asked by non-believers is "What about all the other religions?" How can one say that only one religion leads to God and is ultimately true or superior to all others? Many of us have heard the question, "How can you say that people in other religions are in error if they don't receive and embrace Jesus as their Lord and Savior?" When I am asked the question regarding whether I think Christianity is superior to all religions, I simply answer "yes". Some would say this is being exclusive and narrow-minded. They are right. Christians often feel intimidated by this type of inquisitiveness and interrogation. We rankle at being characterized as possessing a better-than-you attitude or coming across as haughty and arrogant. The conflicts between Christianity and other religions need to be addressed, since we believe that truth, by its nature, is exclusive. In some areas, Christian theology is often diametrically opposed to the teachings of other religions. While most faiths have admiral qualities and aspects about them, none possess the unique credentials of Christianity. We should not be embarrassed or intimidated in declaring with confidence that Jesus and His teachings are on a higher level than any other religious system in the world. All roads do not lead to God. Here are seven reasons that distinguish and set Christianity apart from all other faiths.

1. Offers a comprehensive answer to all aspects of life

Wholesome teachings and moral principles appear in virtually all religions. Such ideal admonitions as "love your fellow man", "do good to your neighbor", "develop a strong family", and "be an honest worker" are all values common to most religions and worth following. However, when comparing Christianity to other religions, C. S. Lewis poignantly puts it this way:

> *If you are a Christian you do not have to believe that all the other religions are simply wrong all through.... But of course being a Christian does mean thinking that where Christianity differs from other religions, Christianity is right and they are wrong.* (C. S. Lewis. *Mere Christianity*, p. 29)

When we advocate that Christianity is matchless among all religions, we mean that the Christian faith is the only one that offers a comprehensive worldview encompassing the issues of God, creation, evil, sin, morality, human worth, salvation, and a future destiny in heaven or hell. All of these themes are chronicled in the Bible. Christianity addresses every key area of life in a complete package that is focused in:

- An all-powerful God Who created with purpose and design,
- A fallen and sinful humanity that is alienated from the Creator, which has polluted the planet with evil and opened the door for the evil kingdom of Satan to operate,
- An historical Savior Who through His life, death, and resurrection has provided a way back to God and a restoration of mankind's dignity, destiny and purpose lost in the Garden of Eden after Adam and Eve's fall,
- A future when God will destroy Satan and all evil, judge the righteous and unrighteousness, and set up the eternal state.

No other religion, except Christianity, is able to comprehensively deal with all these subjects in a unified and coherent fashion. C.S. Lewis puts this in perspective:

> *I believe in Christianity as I believe that the sun has risen; not because I see it, but because by it I see everything else.*

2. Only religion whose founder rose from the dead

Not only is Christianity distinguished in its comprehensive subject matter and scope, it is also the greatest religion because of the bodily resurrection of its founder: Jesus Christ. Many dynamic and powerful religious leaders have lived throughout history. Most of them have made great contributions to life and civilization. However, in terms of worship, spiritual leadership, and teaching, they are inferior to Jesus Christ. As we shall see later, Jesus stated that He was God and could forgive sins. He also declared that He was the only way to God. However, the greatest and most profound claim of Jesus was that He would be killed and after three days rise from the dead.

> *Jesus answered them, "Destroy this temple, and I will raise it again in three days." The Jews replied, "It has taken forty-six years to build this temple, and you are going to raise it in three days?" But the temple he had spoken of was his body.* John 2:19-21

> *From that time on Jesus began to explain to his disciples that he must go to Jerusalem and suffer many things at the hands of the elders, chief priests and teachers of the law, and that he must be killed and on the third day be raised to life.* Matthew 16:21

All that Jesus predicted concerning His death and resurrection came true. Because of this, He is greater in magnitude and accomplishment than any other religious leader. When the teachings of a spiritual leader come into conflict with the instructions of Jesus, they must defer to Him because of His superior credentials. We have a founder Who has risen bodily from the dead. No other religion goes out of its way to even claim this for its founder. The Bible states unequivocally that the resurrection of Christ is the cornerstone of what we preach and an event which makes Christianity unique among the world religions.

This was the clear and unambiguous declaration of the early apostles:

> *Men of Israel, listen to this: Jesus of Nazareth was a man accredited by God to you by miracles, wonders and signs, which God did among you through him, as you yourselves know. This man was handed over to you by God's set purpose and foreknowledge; and you, with the help of wicked men, put him to death by nailing him to the cross. But God raised him from the dead, freeing him from the agony of death, because it was impossible for death to keep its hold on him.* Acts 2:22-24

> *And if Christ has not been raised, our preaching is useless and so is your faith.* 1 Corinthians 15:14.

We noted earlier that Paul, in his defense of Christianity before King Agrippa, used the resurrection of Christ as the key to establishing the credibility and superiority of Christianity (Acts 26:22-28).

3. Establishes a relationship with God based on grace, not works

The third reason that Christianity is set apart from all major religions is that all other prominent faiths, in one form or another, espouse good works and human efforts as a way to earn salvation and a pathway to God. In other words, ones future destiny, however it is defined, is totally shaped and determined by the efforts of the individual. On the contrary, Christianity declares unequivocally that salvation is entirely based on the grace of God alone, manifested in the cross of Christ. It cannot be earned through works and human effort. There is nothing that mankind can attempt to achieve that would be enough to merit God's favor and forgiveness. Works and human efforts hold the key to the future and the present in all major non-Christian religious systems, whether that form be praying five times a day, chanting ritual mantras, or practicing an ascetic and reclusive lifestyle. Contrarily, Christianity asks individuals to receive freely what Jesus has done, not based on their own works or merit, but on God's grace and love. The Bible cannot be any clearer on this topic:

> *If, in fact, Abraham was justified by works, he had something to boast about—but not before God. What does the Scripture say? "Abraham believed God, and it was credited to him as righteousness." Now when a man works, his wages are not credited to him as a gift, but as an obligation. However, to the man who does not work but trusts God who justifies the wicked, his faith is credited as righteousness.* Romans 4:2-5

> *For it is by grace you have been saved, through faith—and this not from yourselves, it is the gift of God—not by works, so that no one can boast.* Ephesians 2:8-9

> *...He saved us, not because of righteous things we had done, but because of his mercy. He saved us through the washing of rebirth and renewal by the Holy Spirit.* Titus 3:5

In Christianity, works are never viewed as the basis for attaining or keeping salvation. Salvation is always pictured as a gift from God incapable of being earned through human merit. Works are viewed in the Bible as the natural product of a love relationship between God and His creation. They are never presented as a way to procure salvation but they do confirm a living faith which abides inside of us. Romans 5:1 declares that we have peace with God (the Greek word *pros* meaning *face-to-face*), not as a result of human endeavors, but through the sacrifice of the Lord Jesus Christ on the cross at Calvary.

> *Therefore, since we have been justified through faith, we have peace with God through our Lord Jesus Christ.* Romans 5:1

4. The primary focus is *worship*, not *teachings*

This is important. All major religions including Islam, Hinduism, and Buddhism focus on adhering to their teachings, laws, and regulations as the key to spiritual attainment in this life and the life to come. On the other hand, Christianity places the emphasis on adhering to teachings in a secondary position to the primary importance of a committed, devoted, and worshipful relationship to the person of Jesus Christ. When the Magi of Christmas fame found the baby Jesus, they presented Him gifts of homage and worshipped Him:

> *On coming to the house, they saw the child with his mother Mary, and they bowed down and worshiped him. Then they opened their treasures and presented him with gifts of gold and of incense and of myrrh.* Matthew 2:11

In fact, throughout His ministry, Jesus was unabashed in calling attention to Himself. John Stott comments on this tendency for Jesus to focus on Himself:

> *The most striking feature of the teaching of Jesus is that he was constantly talking about himself.... This self-centeredness of the teaching of Jesus immediately sets him apart from the other great religious teacher of the world. They were self-effacing, He was self-advancing. They pointed men away from themselves, saying, "That is the truth; so far as I perceive it; follow that." Jesus said, "I am the truth; follow me."* (John Stott, *Basic Christianity*, p. 23)

Jesus made many references to Himself using the personal pronoun *I* in His discourses. Phrases such as *I am the bread of life (John 6:35)*; *I am the light of the world (John 8:12)*; *I am the resurrection and the life (John 11:25-26)*; and *I am the way, the truth and the life (John 14:6)* illustrate the focus on Himself. To many this would appear narcissistic and egotistical, but when one is the Son of God it is very appropriate behavior. If Jesus is not who He said He was, and if he did not do what He said He would do, then He is not worthy of following, even if His teachings have some merit (John 5:39). Jesus invited people to embrace Him personally. He asked his followers to love Him, follow Him and even die for Him. Christianity is more than a *religion*. Above all else, it is a love *relationship* with a Person. This is clearly demonstrated in the book of John, as Jesus invites individuals to partake of Himself:

> *Jesus answered, "Everyone who drinks this water will be thirsty again, but whoever drinks the*

> *water I give him will never thirst. Indeed, the water I give him will become in him a spring of water welling up to eternal life."* John 4:13-14

> *Then Jesus declared, "I am the bread of life. He who comes to me will never go hungry, and he who believes in me will never be thirsty."* John 6:35

> *Just as the living Father sent me and I live because of the Father, so the one who feeds on me will live because of me. This is the bread that came down from heaven. Your forefathers ate manna and died, but he who feeds on this bread will live forever.* John 6:56-58

In another place, the Lord employed the horticultural metaphor of a vine and branch to illustrate His relationship to the disciples:

> *Remain in me, and I will remain in you. No branch can bear fruit by itself; it must remain in the vine. Neither can you bear fruit unless you remain in me.* John 15:4

This personal relationship aspect of Jesus does not diminish the power of His teachings but merely puts them into perspective. We invite individuals into a loving and personal worshipful experience with Jesus first, and then ask them to follow His teachings.

5. A loving, personal, and relational God

Another aspect of Christianity which sets it apart from other faiths is the nature of its God. Most religious gods are often nebulous, impersonal, distant, emotionless, over-demanding or relate to their followers through human effort and religious legalism. The God of Christianity is exactly the opposite. Jehovah of the Bible has always been about covenant relationship with His creation. We learn from the book of Genesis that God walked and talked with Adam and Eve in the Garden of Eden (Genesis 3:8-10). Abraham had the privilege to be depicted as a "friend of God" (James 2:23). The love of God for His people is mentioned numerous times in the Scriptures. The nation of Israel related to Jehovah God in a covenant of love. Notice how the Bible stresses the personal connection of love between God and His people:

> *Because he loved your forefathers and chose their descendants after them, he brought you out of Egypt by his Presence and his great strength.* Deuteronomy 4:37

> *The LORD appeared to us in the past, saying: "I have loved you with an everlasting love; I have drawn you with loving-kindness."* Jeremiah 31:3

The God of Christianity is not distant or remote. He had conversations with Noah, Abraham, Moses, David, Solomon and multitudes of others. The Lord revealed His name, nature and plans to His people, throughout the pages of the Bible. It is no wonder that the one word John uses to define and describe the God of Scripture is love:

And so we know and rely on the love God has for us. God is love. Whoever lives in love lives in God, and God in him. 1 John 4:16

John is not insinuating that God merely has love but is, by definition, love. Love is His nature. John goes further in explaining the application of this love by the fact that God calls us His children:

How great is the love the Father has lavished on us, that we should be called children of God! And that is what we are! The reason the world does not know us is that it did not know him. 1 John 3:1

The Lord even desires to relate to us as a father. The story of the prodigal son in Luke 15 describes God, in the character of the human father, as one Who is compassionate, loving and desirous of a relationship with His children, particularly to those who have fallen away in sin and depravity.

Other religions of the world do not worship this kind of God. Their gods are often detached, distant, and demanding. In Acts 17, Paul even confronted the issue of the "unknown god", while offering hope that the God of creation could be discovered and understood:

Paul then stood up in the meeting of the Areopagus and said: "Men of Athens! I see that in every way you are very religious. For as I walked around and looked carefully at your objects of worship, I even found an altar with this inscription: TO AN UNKNOWN GOD. Now what

> *you worship as something unknown I am going to proclaim to you."* Acts 17:22-23

The God of personal, loving and relational qualities is unique to the Christian faith. The thought that God, in love, would visit this planet through Jesus Christ and provide a way of salvation and a pathway to know Him as Father, is foreign to all other religious systems. The Scripture sums it up well:

> *But God demonstrates his own love for us in this: while we were still sinners, Christ died for us.* Romans 5:8

6. Offers assurance of salvation

Another one of the unique aspects of Christianity is that it offers assurance and certainty regarding salvation, not based on our own effort, but on the finished work of Christ. Since the focus in other religions is based on works and human achievement as a basis of attaining salvation, how would one ever be assured he was doing enough to earn it? When eternity is determined by the works of the individual, there is always going to be a sense of pressure, insecurity and doubt as to whether what we are doing is adequate in terms of substance and quality. This is what makes it frustrating to try and earn salvation through human effort. In contrast, Christianity is based on the finished work of Christ and that alone. Therefore, we can have assurance of salvation because it is not dependent on our own efforts but on the trustworthiness and strength of the Lord. The Bible is clear that it is faith and commitment alone in the finished work of Christ that assures a person of salvation and eternity in heaven (John 3:16-18;

2 Corinthians 5:1-10; 1 John 5:11-12). Paul declared that God was able to guard and keep what the Apostle had entrusted to him:

> *That is why I am suffering as I am. Yet I am not ashamed, because I know whom I have believed, and am convinced that he is able to guard what I have entrusted to him for that day.*
> 2 Timothy 1:12

Paul was referring to his eternal destiny and the final day when salvation will be complete. Since salvation does not rest on human effort or merit, the believer can rest assured that what Christ started in his life at the beginning of salvation, He will bring to completion. This is why the Christian is able face death and, at the same time, have assurance of his future destiny. John writes encouraging words concerning the assurance of salvation and the fact that we can know with certainty we have eternal life:

> *And this is the testimony: God has given us eternal life, and this life is in his Son. He who has the Son has life; he who does not have the Son of God does not have life. I write these things to you who believe in the name of the Son of God so that you may know that you have eternal life.*
> 1 John 5:11-13

Assurance of salvation is based entirely on knowing Christ personally, not upon the amount of effort a believer can demonstrate in his lifetime. This concept is exclusive to the Christian faith and allows all believers the opportunity to live with the assurance and peace that what Jesus started in them, will see its final fruition.

7. Supernaturally empowers its followers

The seventh and final reason why the Christian faith is unique to all other religions is that God internally empowers His followers to accomplish what He asks of them. As stated before, all religions outside of Christianity are based on human effort and work. By the sweat of his brow, man must earn everything his religion gives him through his own ability to keep what is required. The Christian faith is different because what it requires of its followers is provided for internally by God's power through the person of the Holy Spirit. Jesus promised that He would send another (same kind) Helper to be with the disciples and this Helper would dwell in them (John 14:16-18). Later in the chapter, we are told He was referring to the Holy Spirit (John 14:25-26). Before He ascended on high, Jesus assured His disciples that the Holy Spirit would be sent to enable them to be an effective witness for the Lord. This was fulfilled on the Day of Pentecost.

> *But you will receive power when the Holy Spirit comes on you; and you will be my witnesses in Jerusalem, and in all Judea and Samaria, and to the ends of the earth.* Acts 1:8

Paul reinforces this idea in Philippians 2:12-13, where the idea of working out our salvation is coupled with God working in us:

> *Therefore, my dear friends, as you have always obeyed—not only in my presence, but now much more in my absence—continue to work out your salvation with fear and trembling, for it is God*

> *who works in you to will and to act according to his good purpose.* Philippians 2:12-13

True Christian works are never viewed as the sole effort of human sweat but the result of a partnership between God and man. It is interesting in Galatians 5:17-19, Paul distinguishes those characteristics which are the results of human effort (*acts of the sinful nature*) versus those qualities that emanate from the Holy Spirit dwelling in side of us (*fruit of the Spirit*):

> *The acts of the sinful nature are obvious: sexual immorality, impurity and debauchery; idolatry and witchcraft; hatred, discord, jealousy, fits of rage, selfish ambition, dissensions, factions and envy; drunkenness, orgies, and the like. I warn you, as I did before, that those who live like this will not inherit the kingdom of God. But the fruit of the Spirit is love, joy, peace, patience, kindness, goodness, faithfulness....* Galatians 5:19-22

The Greek word translated *acts* in the NIV is *ergon*, which can also be translated *works*. It is translated *works* in the KJV. Fruit is the byproduct of abiding in a source. The contrast could not be clearer. For the follower of Christ, his works and greatest accomplishments are classified as *fruit* which comes internally from the indwelling Holy Spirit, not in human sweat and fleshly efforts. God will reward the believer in eternity for what he allowed the Holy Spirit to accomplish through him, not what he attempted on his own individual human effort.

These seven reasons demonstrate why the Christian faith stands head and shoulders above all other religions. The follower of Christ should never be ashamed to declare them fervently to a needy world.

Comparing Religions Can Be a Healthy Process

Christians will be characterized as unloving if they dare criticize other religions or point out their errors when compared to the Christian faith. However, this process of analyzing and contrasting different religions and faiths can be a very helpful exercise. There are some guidelines which can help us in this process.

Christianity was birthed in a world of many religions
It must be stated that there was an abundance of religious and spiritual activity which existed at the time of Jesus and the first-century church. Jesus incessantly challenged the claims and beliefs of the Jewish religious leaders who objected to His teachings and subverted His ministry by attempting to subjugate the Jewish world to their dangerous practices of strict and oppressive legalism. Ultimately, these Jewish leaders' greatest transgression was rejecting Him as their Messiah. Also, in a time when the Roman emperors were deemed as "gods", Jesus declared Himself to be the true king. It was in the face of this plethora of religion that the Son of God came and declared His uniqueness and invited His followers to abandon all others for Him. Jesus did not mince words that the only pathway to God was through Him and that any other way was specious and in error (John 10:7-10).

In Roman and Greek cultures, a pantheon of gods and temples dotted the geographical landscape imploring their followers to worship a number of deities. As recorded in the book of Acts, Paul journeyed to many cities where pagan temples and shrines to numerous gods were prevalent. Yet, in the midst of these idolatrous religious citadels, he boldly proclaimed the truth of Jesus Christ and His resurrection. When he was done, cities such as Thessalonica, Corinth, Ephesus, and Athens were impacted with the life changing message of Christ. Christian churches were planted in many of these cities.

In addition, it was Paul who challenged the teaching of vain religions and philosophy (Colossians 2:8) and wrote the book of Colossians to counteract the insidious and destructive teachings of the "Gnostic Heresy", a pseudo-Christian movement. This heresy essentially perverted and subverted the essential nature of Christ and His work on the cross as the sole means of salvation.

Remember, in our world of relativity and political correctness, everything is deemed true and valid at the same time. Our so called "enlightened" culture attempts to make all religious teachings equal, regardless of how different or contradictory to each other they might be. However, the New Testament certainly did not espouse a "one size fits all" mentality when it came to religion

Evaluation by comparison is a common practice

Every day we are faced with choices that force us to evaluate whether one product or business is more effective than another. Cell phone and television service companies constantly bombard us with the notion that each is the best company in the world. We generally use factual criteria to support the belief that one product exceeds another in quality, whether we are talking about a car, refrigerator, television, stockbroker, potato chip, or laundry soap. If one can objectively demonstrate superior quality, he has the right to claim that status.

The same is true with religions. As we have discussed, Christianity has credentials which make it greater than any religion on earth, whether Judaism, Islam, Hinduism, or Buddhism. The Christian faith stands up to the tests of truth and passes with flying colors. The Christian should be willing to test the assumption of Christianity's credentials by submitting his faith to rigid standards and objective analysis. The notion that it is wrong to deem another religion inferior is based on the contemporary philosophy that everybody needs to get along and just agree. The truth is that some things are right, and some things are wrong, particularly when it comes to religious thought and teachings. There is nothing wrong with recognizing these distinctions when it comes to religion. After all, eternal destiny is at stake.

Confidence is based on Jesus Christ and Him only

The confidence we possess about our Christian faith does not give us permission to be mean-spirited or nasty toward others with whom we disagree. Our high view of Christianity is entirely based on Jesus Christ Himself, not our own wisdom. Christians have often been guilty of arrogant and haughty attacks on those who differ with them. This is unfortunate. The Christ follower should seek honest debate in the public arena. He ought to defend his faith in the face of strong opposition and attack. However, the Christian should not be arrogant in the process, but exhibit grace and humility. There are many precepts a

Christian can identify with in other religions and there are times when cooperation with other faiths is good and necessary. As Christians, we may disagree with Judaism in terms of their rejection of Christ as the Messiah, but we also must recognize that we share many common beliefs and practices with the Jewish people. Most religions agree on common standards of morality and conduct. Our goal is to persuade others, not pummel them.

One last thought along this line. Christians ought always to recognize the right of others to openly practice their religions and express their beliefs. We live in a free country and religion, in general, is good for a society. If we want the freedom to proclaim our faith in Christ boldly, we must grant that right to others with whom we may disagree.

CHAPTER 6

GOD: ARE YOU OUT THERE?

Rudiment and foundational to Christian theology is the premise that God exists. At this point, it doesn't matter who this God is or what He does; the fact that God exists is essential. The Bible speaks of the necessity of believing in God as a prerequisite for a relationship with Him:

> *And without faith it is impossible to please God, because anyone who comes to him must believe that he exists and that he rewards those who earnestly seek him.* Hebrews 11:6

Unfortunately, many find it hard to believe in the existence of God. *Atheists* contend that a supreme being called "god" does not exist and insists that the world is a product of a non-creator or some random process or event. *Agnostics* believe in the possibility of God's existence, but that neither His existence nor non-existence can be embraced or proven with any certainty. Those who would be classified in the *deist* category maintain belief in a creator but also espouse that this creator is remote and distant. They would advance the idea that God has placed in the human race "natural law" to guide its governance and behavior. Deism was particularly prevalent in the eighteenth century and many of the founding fathers of the United States, such as Thomas Jefferson and Ben Franklin, would have fallen into this category.

The Christian is a *theist*: he believes there is a being called "God" Who was uncaused and is the cause of creation. The Christian theist also maintains that God is active in and with His creation, as opposed to the *deist,* who believes in a God who has isolated Himself from it. We cannot prove the existence of God empirically to someone who will reject everything we say, no matter how persuasive or cogent our logic and arguments might be. However, there are tremendous compelling reasons to support the strong probability of the existence of a supreme being Whom we call "God."

Life without God

Before we enter into a discussion on the arguments for the existence of God, it is helpful to look at the consequences of a world without God. David Lane, a professor of philosophy at Talbot School of Theology, provides a wonderful discussion on this topic. He suggests three dismal consequences in a world without God. (David Lane, *Reasonable Faith*, pp. 72-82)

No ultimate *meaning*

Lane suggests, the first negative consequence for mankind in a world without God is that he loses *ultimate meaning.* Every particular must have a unifying factor to make it worthwhile. A spoke without a wheel has no purpose; a piston without an engine has no reason to exist; likewise, a man without a creator lacks purpose and meaning. Even the atheist Julian Huxley smugly noted, "Man functions better if he thinks there is a God." If man is the ultimate result of chance and is merely a mass of impersonal genes without any creator to define him, he loses ultimate significance for his existence and purpose. Therefore, life is absurd with no purpose or meaningful afterlife. It really doesn't matter whether an individual existed or not, since he lives without meaning and dies the same way. The French existential philosophers Sartre and Camus expressed this in their writings. Sartre summed up man as *adrift in a boat without a rudder on an endless sea.* In a world without God, man is counting the days until he dies and then he drifts into meaningless upon death. As we remove God from our culture, it is no wonder that we are witnessing a generation of humanity desperately searching for meaning and worth, only to come up empty handed. Mankind lives in a dilemma. He desires to have meaning but has eliminated the source of it: God. He seeks identity in the material or even in the spiritual, yet nothing can satisfy his internal conflict like knowing the God Who made him. Schaeffer hits the nail on the head:

> *Every man is in a place of tension. Man cannot make his own universe and then live in it. Thus, Picasso was not able to make his own world, even on his canvas, and be in the position of God, and, at the same time, communicate to the people looking at his painting... Thus, when you face twentieth-century man, whether he is brilliant or any ordinary man of the street, a man of the university or the docks, you are facing a man in tension; and it is this tension which works on*

> *your behalf as you speak to him.... Man today seeks to deflect this tension by saying that he is no more than a machine. If he were no more than a machine he would find no difficulty in proceeding step by step down the line to the logical conclusion of his non-Christian presuppositions. But man is not a machine, even if he says he is.* (Francis Schaeffer. *The God Who Is There*, pp. 122, 124)

Without God, man has no transcendent meaning and few answers for the dilemmas of life. The twentieth century has witnessed more killing and destruction of human life than in all previous history. The moral compass is broken; how can it be fixed when we do not know how to fix it or who can fix it? Once more, Francis Schaeffer sums it up well in speaking of man as created in the image of God:

> *Because God created a true universe outside himself, there is a true history which exists. Man as created in God's image is therefore a significant man in a significant history, who could choose to obey the commandment of God and love him, or revolt against him.... Christianity says man is now abnormal—he is separated from his creator, who is his only sufficient reference point—not by a metaphysical limitation, but by true moral guilt.* (Francis Schaeffer, *The God Who Is There*, pp. 103-104)

The Bible literally shouts from its pages that mankind is special with a valuable identity by declaring that man, from the beginning, was literally made in God's image. No other creatures outside of human beings are depicted as created in God's image. This is reserved for the human race which was uniquely fashioned to reflect who God was:

> *Then God said, "Let us make man in our image, in our likeness, and let them rule over the fish of the sea and the birds of the air, over the livestock, over all the earth, and over all the creatures that move along the ground."* Genesis 1:26

David trumpets the worth of man in the Psalms:

> *O LORD, our Lord, how majestic is your name in all the earth! You have set your glory above the heavens. From the lips of children and infants you have ordained praise because of your enemies, to silence the foe and the avenger. When I consider your heavens, the work of your fingers, the moon and the stars, which you have set in place, what is man that you are mindful of him, the son of man that you care for him? You made him a little lower than the heavenly beings and crowned him with glory and honor. You made him ruler over the works of your hands; you put everything under his feet: all flocks and herds, and the beasts of the field, the birds of the air, and the fish of the sea, all that swim the paths of the seas.* Psalm 8:1-8

Each man's tension is different. We must find what that tension is and appeal to a God Who wants to meet and relieve it.

No ultimate *value*

The second consequence in a world without God, as proposed by Lane, is a loss of value. If there is no God then it really doesn't matter if one has lived a moral or immoral life. There is no one to be accountable to, nobody who defines what is right and wrong and no basis on which to judge the behavior of another. Also, there is no fear of any judgment after this life, since there is not a higher arbitrator of behavior than ourselves and not a concrete definition of what the afterlife would even look like. All the evil acts of men go unpunished and the good deeds of men are unrewarded. We do what we want to do, when we want to do it and however we want to express it.

In a world without God, who is to say that Mother Teresa is any better than Adolph Hitler, or a violent criminal is any more morally upright than a Boy Scout leader? Without God, moral-behavioral definitions are left up to the whims and vagaries of mankind. They can be changed at any time by the will of man. Without God defining the rules, the concept of moral obligation is not clear and ultimately makes no sense. How could anyone have rightly accused Adolph Hitler and his thousands of minions that they were wrong to murder millions of people they deemed valueless, unworthy and inferior, when there is no one above him to define a standard of morality? This is the danger of trying to define a moral code without a moral code giver. We will discuss this in more depth later in this chapter.

No ultimate *purpose*

The third negative effect in a world without God, according to Lane, is that mankind has no ultimate purpose or reason for life. Is man on earth just to live out his life with no end game in mind? If so, he is no different than a gnat or mosquito. If man is a mere product of chance and time (an accident that just happened to occur), he has no basis for purpose or destiny. In essence, as Francis Schaeffer proclaimed, "If God is dead, then man is dead, too." Friedrich Nietzsche, the 19th century German philosopher, is associated with the "God is dead" phenomenon, and the term "nihilism" which meant *the destruction of all meaning and value in life* and was the result of the death-of-God movement. Nietzsche advanced the notion that the end of Christianity would be the advent of nihilism. David Lane tells of Nietzsche's story of the madman who burst on the scene crying, "I seek God! I seek God!" After receiving the taunts of the audience, who did not believe in the existence of God, the madman proclaimed:

> *"Whither is God?" he cried, "I shall tell you. We have killed him—you and I.... God is dead.... And we have killed him. How shall we, the murderers of all murderers comfort ourselves?"* (David Lane, *Reasonable Faith*, p.77)

When God created Adam and Eve, He formed them with purpose, meaning and value. They were the only living creatures made in the image of God. Because of this distinction, they knew who they were and why they were created. They had a purpose and meaning for life in a context of the relationship that existed with their Creator. Things changed as they bought into the lie, suggested by the evil creature (serpent), that they would experience even greater meaning and value if they acted independently and rebelliously toward the God Who created them. It is important to observe that *in trying to become something they already were, a people with purpose and meaning, they became something they were never intended to be: insecure and suffering the ravages of sin*. After their disobedience, Adam and Eve found out quickly that the serpent had lied to them and their act of perfidy and independence from their Creator brought them much misery and pain. Satan is perpetrating the same lie today to a world gullible and willing to believe this insidious message. And like Adam and Eve, by moving away from God, mankind is suffering the same devastating consequences the original humans experienced many years ago: a loss of meaning, value, and purpose.

Arguments for the Existence of God

A world without God creates numerous insoluble and perplexing problems for the human race. The only hope for our world is that God exists and has created each person with dignity, meaning, value and worth. However, the idea of God's existence is being challenged by many in our modern culture. Generations of young people are receiving education, particularly in institutions of higher learning, from atheistic professors who often, with evangelistic fervor (particularly in the science disciplines) dismiss the idea of God's existence as poppycock and balderdash. Globally renowned atheists such as Richard Dawkins, Sam Harris, and Daniel Dennett have become very aggressive both in print and media in advocating and advancing the case for atheism. Therefore, it is important to discuss the many powerful reasons that suggest the strong probability that God does exist and challenge our skeptical and incredulous culture in this area.

The cosmological or cause/contingency argument

The cosmological argument for the existence of God, based on first cause and contingency, has been proffered and refined by Christian apologists for centuries. Over the years, great thinkers, such as the eminent Catholic theologian Thomas Aquinas and the German mathematician and philosopher G.W.F Leibniz, have advanced technical explanations of this approach to prove the existence of God. Aquinas argued that anything moving has been moved by something else and that one must ultimately conclude there is a first mover who did not have to be moved by anyone outside of itself. This argument maintains that every event in the universe has a cause. Matter cannot create itself. Logically, there has to be a first cause that did not need to be caused. This first cause is what we call "god". The process must begin somewhere. Professor Dallas Willard says:

> *However concrete physical reality is sectioned, the result will be a state of affairs which owes its being to something other than itself... in that series of causes there has to be at least one state of being which itself exists but does not derive its existence from anything else. It is self-existent, i.e., uncaused.* (Dallas Willard. *Theistic Defense,* cited by Ravi Zecharias in *Can Man Live Without God?* p. 191)

Norman Geisler states it this way:

> *The theist need not claim that everything has a cause.... Rather, he can return to the Thomistic principle of existential causality which claims that every finite, contingent, and changing*

> *thing has a cause. If this principle is sound and leads to an infinite, necessary, and unchanging Being, then this Being will not need a cause. God will be the Uncaused Cause of everything else that exists.* (Norman Geisler. *Christian Apologetics,* p. 238)

This is very logical. The probability of something physically existing from nothing is zero. This is recognized today by both the scientific and non-scientific world. Not a single physical state or event is known to have originated from nothing. Therefore, there has to be a non-caused cause to start the cycle. Secular science often proffers an idea like the "big-bang theory" to be this non-caused cause. In fact, it replaces God. Dallas Willard addresses this view:

> *That "bang" is often treated as if it were not quite or not just a physical event, as indeed it could not be. But what, then, could it be? Enter "scientific mysticism." And we must at least point out that an eternally self-subsistent being is no more improbable than a self-subsistent event emerging from no cause.* (Dallas Willard. *Theistic Defense,* cited by Ravi Zecharias in *Can Man Live without God?* p. 192)

One of the world's most renowned and famous scientists, Stephen Hawking, brings the question into rational light:

> *The odds against a universe like ours emerging out of something like the Big Bang are enormous.... I think there are clearly religious implications whenever you start to discuss the origins*

> *of the universe. There must be religious overtones. But I think most scientists prefer to shy away from the religious side of it.* (Cited by Robert C. Newman, chapter 2.2, in John Warwick Montgomery, *Evidence For Faith*, p. 68)

In the book of Hebrews, we are told that to come to God, we must believe that He is. This first cause fits the idea of what we call God: Someone Who did not need to be caused and thus had the power to create. The Bible supports this argument:

> *In the beginning God created the heavens and the earth.* Genesis 1:1

> *...since what may be known about God is plain to them, because God has made it plain to them. For since the creation of the world God's invisible qualities—his eternal power and divine nature—have been clearly seen, being understood from what has been made, so that men are without excuse.* Romans 1:19-20

> *The heavens declare the glory of God; the skies proclaim the work of his hands.* Psalms 19:1

Apart from this eternal being, mankind has to come up with another explanation for the creation of the physical universe and this is usually some spontaneous natural cause. It takes more faith to believe that such a colossal event as the creation of the universe could emerge from no cause than it does to believe in an eternal, self-subsistent being. C. S. Lewis aptly expressed it this way:

An egg which came from no bird is no more natural than a bird which had existed from all eternity. (C. S. Lewis, *God in the Dock,* p. 211)

Teleological or design argument

Complexity logically leads one to conclude that some intelligent force had to design it. This is the essence of the Teleological argument for the existence of God. This approach has become more prominent as recent scientific discoveries have demonstrated the complexity of organisms and cells, as well as the breathtaking advancements in genetics as it relates to the the human body. Quantum physics has introduced a whole new dimension concerning the nature of the physical universe and the behavior of matter and energy on the atomic and subatomic level. Order and design presuppose thought and a designer. Whether we are speaking of a computer with hundreds of components, a skyscraper with magnificent designs, the human body with its complex genetic code, or the vastness of the universe and all intricate aspects which comprise it, it is reasonable to conclude that some intelligent force lay behind it all.

Scientific discoveries have taken us way beyond the point of just accepting these detailed aspects of life as the mere product of random chance. Try setting a monkey at a keyboard and see if a book or manuscript is produced, or a wonderful opera and musical set is composed. Order necessitates that a unique and formidable intelligence must precede it. *Design in mind precedes design in kind.* This fits our view of God. It doesn't take a lot of intelligence to conclude that complex organisms must have a complex designer. Yet, it is amazing in our world of secularism and skepticism toward spiritual dimensions, particularly God and faith, that many would attribute the complex nature of our universe to random chance and lengthy processes that do not include a creator.

On the other hand, the theist (specifically those of Judeo-Christian beliefs) espouse unequivocally this designer is God. When we observe our planet, we see incredible aspects of it that cannot logically be explained apart from a supreme creator and designer. John MacArthur discusses the incredible design and uniqueness of our earth:

> *At any given time, there are an average of 1800 storms in operation in the world. The energy needed to generate those storms amounts to the incredible figure of 1,300,000,000 horsepower. By comparison, a large earth-moving machine has 420 horsepower and requires a hundred gallons of fuel a day to operate. Just one of those storms, producing a rain of four inches over an area of ten thousand square miles, would require energy equivalent to the burning of 640,000,000 tons of coal to evaporate enough water for such a rain. And to cool those vapors and collect them in clouds would take another 800,000,000 horsepower of refrigeration working night and day for a hundred days.*
>
> *Agricultural studies have determined that the average farmer in Minnesota gets 407,510 gallons of rainwater per acre per year, free of charge, of course. The state of Missouri has some 70,000 square miles and averages 38 inches of rain a*

year. That amount of water is equal to a lake 250 miles long, 60 miles wide, and 22 feet deep.

The US Natural Museum has determined that there are at least 10 million species of insects, including some 2,500 varieties of ants. There are about 5 billion birds in the United States, among which are some species able to fly 500 miles non-stop across the Gulf of Mexico. Mallard ducks can fly 60 miles an hour, eagles 100 miles an hour, and falcons can dive at speeds of 180 miles an hour.

The earth is 25,000 miles in circumference, weighs 6 septillion, 588 sextillion tons, and hangs unsupported in space. It spins at 1,000 miles per hour with absolute precision and careens through space around the sun at the speed of 1,000 miles per minute in an orbit 580 million miles long.

The human heart is about the size of its owner's fist. An adult heart weighs less than half a pound, yet can do enough work in twelve hours to lift 65 tons one inch off the ground. A water molecule is composed of only three atoms. But if all the molecules in one drop of water were the size of a grain of sand, they could make a road one foot thick and a half mile wide that would stretch from Los Angeles to New York. Amazingly, however, the atom itself is largely space, its actual matter taking up only one trillionth of its volume. (John MacArthur. *The MacArthur New Testament Commentary: Romans 1-8,* pp. 80-81)

How can one even imagine the myriad of interactions necessary for the human eye to see or the complexities of a human birth to happen, could have come about by chance or natural selection? Scripture defines creation as the handiwork of God. It is a beautiful product emanating from an intelligent designer:

> *The heavens declare the glory of God; the skies proclaim the work of his hands.* Psalms 19:1

> *For since the creation of the world God's invisible qualities—his eternal power and divine nature—have been clearly seen, being understood from what has been made, so that men are without excuse.* Romans 1:20

During the last several decades we have witnessed a flurry of discussions and debates revolving around the subject of "intelligent design". Many scientists are becoming mathematically compelled to admit that there must be some force outside of us that designed the intricate dimensions we are witnessing in the universe and the human body. In a way, secular science has cannibalized itself because, the more science discovers about the mathematical complexity of the universe, the more likely it is that someone created and designed it. A great example of this is the astonishing admission by one of the world's former leading atheists: Anthony Flew.

Admission from a leading atheist

Antony Flew, a prominent English philosopher who is now deceased, had been recognized for decades as an icon to atheists around the world. Flew had taught at such prestigious universities such as Oxford, Aberdeen, Keel and Reading, as well as York University in Toronto. However, in 2004, something dramatic and astonishing occurred in Flew and he became a deist. Based on scientific evidence, he changed his mind concerning the existence of God. An article by the associated press on December 9, 2004 explains what happened:

> *A British philosophy professor who has been a leading champion of atheism for more than a half-century has changed his mind. He now believes in God more or less based on scientific evidence, and says so on a video released Thursday.*
>
> *At age 81, after decades of insisting belief is a mistake, Anthony Flew has concluded that some sort of intelligence or first cause must have created the universe. A super-intelligence is the only good explanation for the origin of life and the complexity of nature, Flew said in a telephone interview from England.* (Associated press article taken from the website, www.abcnews.go.com? US? wire Story, 2005)

Flew, who did an extensive interview with *Christianity Today* magazine, admitted he did not follow the God of Christianity and is much like a deist in the manner of Thomas Jefferson. However, the fact that he even came to the conclusion that God existed is a startling admission by a man once adamant that there was no supreme intelligence or creator. Flew had to be honest that the complexity of our world is a compelling argument for the existence of God.

Mathematics make the case for an "intelligent designer"

Another example of intelligent design comes from the work of Dr. David Foster, a mathematician, scientist, and engineer who was associated with leading scientists at Cambridge, England, during the Einstein era before WWII. At King's College in London, he worked with Alex Ivanhoff, the first person to give an adequate description of the cybernetic law of negative feedback control. Later, he assisted Sir Frank Whittle in developing the first jet engine. In his book, *Does God Exist?*, he uses the example of the 564 numerical properties of 20 amino acid types necessary to form hemoglobin, which is the main protein in red blood. In calculating the mathematical probability for all of these amino acid types to come together perfectly by chance is $P=10^{564.}$ This is an immense number, 10 multiplied by itself 564 times. Without getting into too much detail, this is a number which is impossible to be reached by chance. It speaks of an "intelligent designer." (Material taken from an article in the *Saturday Evening Post*, Nov. Dec. 1999, pp 59ff.)

Science makes the case for an "intelligent design" viewpoint

Logic and science support the view that this world and its inhabitants are the products of an "intelligent designer", not of chance. Recently, we have seen an increase of scientists who are fostering and promoting the idea of "intelligent design". These scientists do not approach the issue from a religious perspective but from a scientific one. They believe scientific conclusions should follow the facts and not be based on dogmatic, preconceived ideas. In their view, the complexity of cells and the mechanisms within them, make it highly unlikely that these forms could have developed apart from an intelligent designer.

One of these scientists is Dr. Michael J. Behe, a professor of biochemistry at Lehigh University, who published a book challenging classical Darwinian evolution entitled *Darwin's Black Box.* In 2008, I heard Dr. Behe lecture on the subject of "intelligent design". The center piece of his argument is the "bacterial flagellum", which is attached to each cell surface. It is also attached to, and rotated by, an electrical motor made of (40) different proteins. All of these proteins must be present for the flagellum to function properly. Dr. Behe uses the flagellum to speak of the concept of "irreducible complexity", which means that if a structure is so complex all of its parts must initially be present for it to function properly. It is to be irreducibly complex. Dr. Behe maintains all of the parts of a bacterial flagellum must have been present from the beginning in order to function, not gradually over time. In commenting on Behe's viewpoint, Dr. Dudley Eirich, himself a microbiologist states:

> *This contradicts the evolutionary theory that any component which doesn't offer an advantage to an organism will be lost or discarded. How such a structure could have evolved in a gradual, step-by-step process as required by classical Darwinian evolution is an insurmountable obstacle to evolutionist.* (Dr Eirich quote taken from an article from www.answeringgenesis.org website, 3/30/2003)

Classic evolution has no explanation for this. This example and many more which could be cited, clearly raise the necessity for a Designer of the universe.

Moral or values argument

Perhaps the greatest argument for the existence of God can be found in the moral argument. Man's awareness of right and wrong points to a supreme lawgiver. If we believe that evil exists, then we logically must believe good also exists, since evil by definition is the opposite of good. The existence of good and evil requires a moral law from which to differentiate between the two. If we have a moral law, we must have a moral lawgiver. Again, these conditions affirm the existence of God. C. S. Lewis in his seminal book, *Mere Christianity*, brilliantly expounds on this thought:

> *There are two points I want to make. First, that human beings, all over the earth, have this curious idea that they ought to behave in a certain way, and cannot really get rid of it. Secondly, that they do not in fact behave in that way. They know the Law of Nature; they break it. These two facts are the foundation of all clear thinking about ourselves and the universe we live in. The moment you say that one set of moral ideas can be better than another; you are, in fact, measuring them both by a standard, saying that one of them conforms to that standard more nearly than the other.* (C. S. Lewis. *Mere Christianity*, p. 7)

There is a common universal understanding that some things are right and some things are wrong. It is as if God has placed in every human being a moral DNA or standard that represents God's values and moral code. The Bible speaks to this issue. Not only is morality inscribed in Scripture, it is also written on the heart of every human. All humanity has a sense of right and wrong. This sense comes from the supreme lawgiver: God.

> *Indeed, when Gentiles, who do not have the law, do by nature things required by the law, they are a law for themselves, even though they do not have the law, since they show that the requirements of the law are written on their hearts, their consciences also bearing witness, and their thoughts now accusing, now even defending them.* Romans 2:14-15

C. S. Lewis elucidates on this thought:

> *You find out more about God from the Moral Law than from the universe in general just as you find out more about a man by listening to his conversation than by looking at a house he has built. Now, from this second bit of evidence we conclude that the Being behind the universe is intensely interested in right conduct—in fair play, unselfishness, courage, good faith, honesty, and truthfulness. In that sense, we should agree with the account given by Christianity and some other religions, that God is good.* (C. S. Lewis. *Mere Christianity*, p. 17)

If we come to the conclusion that there are indeed moral values which emanate from a Supreme Lawgiver, we refer to as God, then the question is ultimately: what is our responsibility to those values? David Lane discusses the difference between a moral value and a moral duty:

> *When we speak of moral values, we're talking about whether something is good or bad; when we talk about moral duties, we are concerned about whether something is right or wrong. Although we are apt to equate what is right with what is good and what is wrong with what is bad, a little reflection reveals this to be mistaken. Right and wrong have to do with moral obligation, what I ought or ought not to do. But obviously, I am not morally obligated to do something just because it would be good for me to do it. For example, it's a good thing to become a chemist, but that doesn't imply that is therefore my duty to become a chemist.... To say that there are objective moral values is to say that something is good or evil independently of whether any human being believes it to be so. Similarly, to say that we have objective moral duties is to say that certain actions are right or wrong for us independently of whether any human being believes them to be so.* (David Lane, *A Reasonable Faith*, p.172)

The existence of God helps us not only to know what is right and wrong but also whether we should do or not do certain things. This is an *objective* position, not a *subjective* one. Moral values and duties are not subject to the subjective whims of a human or group; they exist outside of us and belong to the realm of God. Without God, it is left up to mankind to capriciously decide what is right and wrong and to determine whether he is obligated to even abide by those values. This is a very dangerous proposition for our world that has witnessed devastating consequences for humanity, particularly in the twentieth and twenty-first centuries. Hitler and his Nazi minions defined what was right and wrong and what was good and evil. Murder was justified in the name of the "master race". They were accountable to no one else but their own ideology and political party. Because of this subjective man-centered morality, millions of human beings lost their lives and millions more suffered untold hardships and tragedies. Without God, who determines the immutable moral values and duties? What right would anyone have to tell Hitler he was wrong?

Thermodynamics or entropy argument

Another argument for the existence of God centers around the second law of thermodynamics which, in its simplest form, states that energy in a closed system will eventually tend toward a state of equilibrium. This means that unless energy is continually fed into the system, the processes in the system will run down and stop functioning. For instance, a gasoline tank is a closed energy system. It will run out of fuel unless someone outside the system puts more gasoline in it. This is an example of the second law of thermodynamics which defines entropy. The eminent scientist Henry Morris comments on the law of increased entropy:

> *Also known as the Law of Increasing Entropy, this Second Law is now recognized as a universal law of science, with no known exception ever observed. It says, quite simply, that every system tends to become disordered, to run down*

> *and eventually die. Its entropy, which is a measure of disorder, always tends to increase.* (Henry Morris. *Many Infallible Proofs*, p. 88)

The world is an energy source, but why hasn't the universe run out of energy? The sun is an energy source, but why hasn't it manifested the results of a decreasing energy supply? Why is it that, for thousands or even millions of years, according to some, we have not witnessed a consistent diminishing expression of energy necessary to sustain our planet?

David Lane raises the same question as he applies the second law of thermodynamics to cosmology:

> *Now our interest in the law is what happens when it is applied to the universe as a whole. For the universe is, on the atheistic view, a gigantic closed system, since it is everything there is and there is nothing outside it.... If in a finite amount of time the universe will inevitably come to equilibrium, from which no significant further change is physically possible, then it should already be at equilibrium by now, if it has existed for infinite time. Like a ticking clock, it should by now have run down. Since it has not yet run down, this implies, in the words of Richard Schlegel, that "in some way the universe must have been wound up."* (David Lane, *Reasonable Faith*, p. 141.)

This presents insoluble problems for the atheist who claims that the universe is a closed system, since there is no existing force outside of it necessary to sustain it.

Yet, the planet shows no sign of running out of energy. The reason the earth and the sun continue to function at normal energy levels is because something or someone outside of the universe sustains them and maintains their energy levels. The Christian believes there is a God-force Who allows it to function at a high energy level. Science and logic should lead us to the conclusion that there must be someone outside our planet who is this sustaining power. We know that the earth is not eternal; therefore it cannot sustain itself. The Bible reveals to us clearly Who does sustain the universe: Jesus Christ.

> *The Son is the radiance of God's glory and the exact representation of his being, sustaining all things by his powerful word.* Hebrews 1:3

The word translated *sustaining* is from the Greek verb *pherō*, which in essence means *to bear* or *carry*. Often in the New Testament *pherō* is translated *to support* or *bear up under*. As it pertains to the universe, F.F. Bruce states:

> *Jesus upholds the universe, not like Atlas supporting a dead weight on his shoulders, but as One who carries all things forward on their appointed course.* (F.F. Bruce, NIC-Hebrews, p.6)

Jesus, Who helped create the world, will make sure that this planet functions properly until the day Christ returns to make all things new. In another place the Apostle Paul writes:

> *He is before all things, and in him all things hold together.* Colossians 1:17

The Greek word translated *hold together* is from *sunistēmi*, conveying the idea of *holding something together*, thus sustaining it. Jesus, Who existed before the world He created, is the one Who holds the universe together. In essence, God is the reason that the earth and the sun do not run out of energy and have continued to operate at consistent life giving levels for thousands of years.

One day, according to Scripture, the earth will fall apart and disintegrate when the Lord removes His hand from sustaining its processes. Peter in his epistle describes the result of this:

> *By the same word the present heavens and earth are reserved for fire, being kept for the day of judgment and destruction of ungodly men.... But the day of the Lord will come like a thief. The heavens will disappear with a roar; the elements will be destroyed by fire, and the earth and everything in it will be laid bare... as you look forward to the day of God and speed its coming. That day will bring about the destruction of the heavens by fire, and the elements will melt in the heat.* 2 Peter 3:7, 10, 12

The translation, *will be destroyed by fire* is made up of two Greek words. The first is *kusoomai*, a word which was employed by medical writers to express *feverish heat*. Here the word seems to indicate intense, internal heat, perhaps like that of a volcano (Fritz Rienecker, *Linguistic Key to the New Testament*, p.782). The second word is *luō,* which means *to loose* or *untie.* The indication here is that all the elements will be violently separated from each other. The earth will come apart or unravel in a dramatic, violent fashion. What a vivid depiction of the end of the world. All God has to do is take His finger off this planet and it will dramatically come apart and be destroyed. The good news is that one day there will a new earth, perfectly fashioned and created by God. This is what followers of Christ will enjoy after the Lord returns. John conveys this in the book of Revelation:

> *Then I saw a new heaven and a new earth, for the first heaven and the first earth had passed away, and there was no longer any sea.*
> Revelation 21:1

Christological argument

Another cogent argument for the existence of God is none other than Jesus Christ Himself. Jesus walked this earth in a human body and at the same time unabashedly and openly claimed to be God. The disciples, who chronicled His life and ministry, in unison affirm that their Messiah was indeed Jehovah God of the Old Testament. If we substantiate Jesus as a historical person and believe He factually did rise from the dead, then we have a historical demonstration of God, which provides evidence that He exists. Of course, this argument can only be adduced by those who believe that Jesus Christ did indeed walk the earth and was the person He claimed to be as chronicled in Holy Scripture.

There are two ways to describe a person or an event. One way is to use phrases and details to communicate to someone else what you are trying to get across. For instance, if I want to depict someone's face, I could use such terms as blue eyes, brown hair and a round nose.

These words may not convey the ideal description since a great many people possess these characteristics. However, there is a second way to describe someone. If I say, "My friend looks like Abraham Lincoln," this description communicates volumes. What I have done is compared my friend to someone with whom the listener is familiar.

In describing God, we can use an abundance of words and phrases to get across what He is like or we can simply point to Jesus and say, "God is like Him." You see, the uniqueness of the Christian God is that He openly reveals Himself in ways that we can identify with. Jesus was someone Who manifested the character and power of God in a human body. If we truly desire to know what God is like, we just have to point to Jesus. The Bible unequivocally declares that Jesus was God and manifested the characteristics of God in His life:

> *In the beginning was the Word, and the Word was with God, and the Word was God.* John 1:1

> *No one has ever seen God, but God the One and Only, who is at the Father's side, has made him known.* John 1:18

> *Jesus answered: "Don't you know me, Philip, even after I have been among you such a long time? Anyone who has seen me has seen the Father. How can you say, 'Show us the Father.'?"* John 14:9

The non-Christian cannot escape this fact. All he can do is try and discredit the historicity of Jesus by impugning the integrity and accuracy of the primary documents: the New-Testament books which chronicle His life from birth to resurrection. The person of Jesus Christ creates insurmountable problems for the skeptic because His life was indeed the personification of the character, nature and power of God. If Christ did indeed exist and perform all the miracles and astonishing things in His life the Bible records, especially rising from the dead, then He is a compelling argument for the existence of God. We will discuss this subject in greater detail in our chapter on Christ.

These arguments for the evidence of God cannot prove the existence of a Supreme Being or Creator to a skeptic, but they highly suggest the probability and necessity of such a force to exist. They also point out the difficulties of trying to explain the complex aspects of the universe without Him. Apart from God, we are forced to make sense of a world with illogical and unreasonable paradigms that stretch the imagination and force us to accept, indefensible explanations. It makes more sense and requires less faith to believe in a world where God exists, than a world where He does not.

What does God look like? Jesus

CHAPTER 7

GOD IS OUT THERE: LET'S MEET HIM

In our logical progression, if we accept the existence of a Supreme Being, Who is responsible for creating this universe, what good does it do if we cannot identify and know Him? What is the point in acknowledging there is a "god" behind this universe when we don't know a thing about Him, precluding any possibility of a relationship? This is what makes *deism* so untenable. Why would God take the time to create the universe with so many amazing details, including mankind, and just walk away as if He didn't care. Believing in a "god" is an essential first step toward a spiritual journey, however, this is not enough. James in his epistle indicates, that even reprehensible demons believe in the existence of God (James 2:19). The world not only needs to know that God exists, but it is also important to understand that He is vitally interested in them personally and can be discovered and embraced. He also possesses a name and has a very unique nature and character. Communicating all of this to a skeptical and secular culture is a daunting task.

When one mentions the idea of "god" in our modern world, it can engender many varied responses. To those who do believe that God exists (as opposed to the atheist who does not, or the agnostic who is not sure) their concept of God can range from someone who is distant and unknowable, to one who is over-demanding, legalistic, harsh, oppressive and vindictive. Many religious groups would define "god" as one with the universe in a pantheistic sense, making their god virtually indistinguishable from the creation. The challenging task for the Christian is to effectively present to his culture the God of Scripture, as chronicled in the Old Testament and manifested in the life and work of Jesus Christ. This involves counteracting and challenging the erroneous views of God which exist primarily in the area of religious thought. We are provided a great example of how to accomplish this in the Bible. Let's travel to Athens.

Paul Goes to Mars Hill

In Acts 17, Luke records the account of how the Apostle Paul confronted the philosophers of Athens with the truths of the God of Christianity. In many ways, our modern culture is parallel to that which Paul faced in Athens. We are a very educated and scholarly society with many varied views of religion and philosophies that dominate our thinking. Also, in Athens the precepts of Christianity were very foreign to these scholars and to their culture in general. In the same way, in our modern society, Christianity is becoming less and less familiar as secular forces seek to marginalize and remove the Bible, Christ and the God of Scriptures from all aspects of our lives. This meeting took place on Mars Hill (Areopagus), which was the gathering place for the intellectually elite in Athens.

One of the gods in Athens, which particularly caught Paul's attention, was even titled an *unknown god* (Acts 17:23). Athens can be described as a wealthy and intellectual city that placed a premium on intellect and reason. The city was a blend of superstitious idolatry and enlightened philosophy. There were two prevalent philosophies in the thinking of these Athenian scholars and philosophers Paul faced on Mars Hill. Luke records them:

> *A group of Epicurean and Stoic philosophers began to dispute with him. Some of them asked, "What is this babbler trying to say?"* Acts 17:18

Epicureanism

The first major philosophy was *Epicureanism*, whose adherents believed the gods, if they existed, were very distant and had nothing to do with human beings. In this sense they were similar to the deists. In their view, the gods didn't require or demand anything from us, consequently, we need not fear any judgment from them. Epicureans lived quiet and happy lives. Part of their philosophy was that we should moderate our desires, to do nothing that would feed our natural hopes or fears. They believed the ideal life was one uncluttered with complicated questions regarding one's destiny and matters related to god. The popular phrase, "Eat, drink and be merry for tomorrow we die" is attributed to the Epicurean way of life. However, this was not meant to be taken in a debaucherously or hedonistic way, but was a simple statement of life.

Stoicism

The second major philosophical force Paul addressed in Athens was *Stoicism*, which was the polar opposite to Epicureanism. The Stoics believed in many gods and were pantheistic, in that they embraced the idea that god and the world were essentially the same. They maintained there was a divine life in all human beings. Thus, Stoics were much more religious than the Epicureans.

It was to this diverse and inquisitive group of thinkers and scholars that Paul targeted his famous and powerful address. The Apostle Paul was disturbed when he observed that Athens was full of idols (Acts 17:16). He immediately asked for an audience so that he could bring truth and clarity about the Christian God to the minds of these scholars. It is interesting to note that the Apostle did not buy into the common notion, prevalent in our day, that it doesn't matter which god one worships or religion he participates in because all of them eventually lead to the same conclusion of eternal blessing. It is important to analyze the principles about God and Christianity that Paul used to communicate to these Athenian scholars. We will discover many relevant parallels to our own time.

Meet the God of Christianity

As we stated earlier, it is not only important to believe that God exists, but also to discover Who He is, what He is like, and how He relates to us. In his epic address to these stodgy and high-minded philosophers on Mars Hill (Areopagus), Paul lays out the case for the Christian God by describing His nature and character in a powerful and detailed way. This was certainly a message they had never heard before.

God can be and desires to be known

The first principle about the Christian God that Paul desired these intellectual elites to grasp was that the He was knowable. Here, Paul is addressing the Epicureans who believed that God was remote and virtually unknowable. The impetus for Paul to communicate this idea was provoked by the presence of the altar to the *unknown god* which Paul observed as he was walking through Athens.

> *For as I walked around and looked carefully at your objects of worship, I even found an altar with this inscription: TO AN UNKNOWN GOD. Now what you worship as something unknown I am going to proclaim to you.* Acts 17:23

The Apostle contrasts the ambiguous and anonymous nature of this unknown god with the definable and descript God he worshipped. Many today believe in the existence of some supreme being but find him indiscernible or remotely distant. In many ways, even those in our society who believe in a God, know very little about what He is like. If they pray, they pray to a God with whom they have no relationship. Much like the Athenians, they worship at the altar of the "Unknown God". Like the deists in the seventeenth and eighteenth centuries, some people have a hard time connecting the idea of a god to any personal or relevant situation. This raises the question, "What good is it to believe in a god who is virtually undefinable and has little relevance to one's life or circumstances?"

Recently, the body of an unknown soldier was exhumed to determine his true identity. Understandably, the family felt it much better to have a grave with a name on it than an anonymous tomb. The same attitude should be true in our quest to know God. The good news for the skeptic is that the God of the Bible does not have to be anonymous, because He is very knowable and definable. He has a name, personality, volition, and His acts and exploits are chronicled in recorded history throughout the pages of Scripture. This is good news for mankind. Paul made it very clear: God can be known and, more importantly, desires to be known.

God has revealed Himself to the world through three primary avenues:

1. *Natural Revelation* - He has made His character and nature known through creation. This is also called "natural revelation". Paul alludes to this in Romans 1:20-22, as he appeals to mankind's basic sense of sight and observation of the heavenly bodies to at least ask questions about someone who might have created such an awesome universe.

2. *Incarnational Revelation* - God has revealed Himself through the person of Jesus Christ. This is "incarnational revelation". When Philip asked the Lord to show him the Father, Jesus replied, "Anyone who has seen me has seen the Father." (John 14:9) Jesus Christ was God revealed in a human body. In John 12:45, Jesus indicated that, when a person looked at Him, He was also seeing the One Who sent Him, referring to God the

Father. He spoke the way that God would speak and did the things that God would do. In Jesus' human body, God made a way for all who witnessed and heard Him to tangibly experience the living God.

3. *Special Revelation* - God has also communicated Himself throughout the pages of Scripture. This is "special revelation". The entire Bible is virtually a chronicle of God's interactions with His people. From Adam, Abraham, Moses to the prophets, we witness the Lord revealing His name and character, while talking with, guiding and loving His people. During Moses encounter with God at the burning bush, Moses asked Him to reveal His name. The Lord replied:

   Moses said to God, "Suppose I go to the Israelites and say to them, 'The God of your fathers has sent me to you,' and they ask me, 'What is his name?' Then what shall I tell them?" God said to Moses, "I AM WHO I AM. This is what you are to say to the Israelites: 'I AM has sent me to you.'" Exodus 3:13-14

   In the name *I AM*, God was defining himself as the *One who always was, is,* and *ever will be*. We understand this name more readily in the sacred appellation, *Jehovah*. God would be the ever present One for His people. The Scriptures are a revelation of God's attributes and nature. They speak of His love, righteousness, holiness, fairness, and power. There is no other book like the Bible when it comes to describing the nature of God. It is not enough just to admit to the possibility of

God's existence, it is as equally important to discover His name and characteristics as well.

God is the Creator of the universe and separate from it

In the face of the Stoic pantheistic views of his audience, Paul was unabashed in proclaiming that his God was the Creator of everything, yet separate from it.

> *The God who made the world and everything in it is the Lord of heaven and earth....* Acts 17:24

When Paul attributed the existence of this world as a creative act of God, he was automatically separating the creation from the Creator. This declaration would not go over well today in our culture. Modern man is guided by viewpoints that attribute the existence of this planet to the "big-bang theory" or another non-theistic creative process. Today, classic Darwinian evolution is the worldview underlying most discussions of anthropology and the origin of life. More faith is required to believe in this non-theistic theory than to believe in an all-powerful Creator. Paul boldly presents God as the Creator of this planet.

He declares God is the Lord over the heavens and the earth because He created it. The term *Lord, kurios*, is used here in the sense of one who is a *master, ruler* or *a superior.* This is tantamount to saying that no other god can compare with the God of the Bible. The earth is not God and God is not the earth. They are related but distinct from each other. Our modern world is full of Eastern religious thought which fosters the notion that God is not separate from His creation. This has led to extreme environmental positions regarding the earth and animals. This pantheistic idea is diametrically opposed to the teaching of the Bible. The Creator-God has no rivals and the earth is His domain. This truth contradicts the common notion today that all "gods" are equal. Paul's approach to the concept of "god" was that the God of the Bible was the one true God, responsible for all of creation and worthy of homage from it. True meaning and value in life can only be found by going back to the original source of creation: the God of the Scripture.

God is boundless and uncontainable

The Greek world was full of temples dedicated to their various gods. Temples were considered places where the pagan gods and idols who defined them resided. The place the worshipper could meet these gods where in manmade, physical shrines. Paul addresses this issue head on with a powerful statement regarding the uncontained nature of his God:

> *...does not live in temples built by hands.* Acts 17:24

Paul's God cannot be bound by any physical object or image residing in a temple. He is truly uncontainable and immense. God is everywhere at all times (omnipresent) and, according to Paul, does not reside in man-made temples. In Pauline theology, what makes the God of Christianity so unique is that He has chosen His Church, comprised of Christ followers, to be His temple, instead of edifices of brick and stone. Paul makes this clear in his epistles:

> *Don't you know that you yourselves are God's temple and that God's Spirit lives in you? If anyone destroys God's temple, God will destroy him; for God's temple is sacred, and you are that temple.* 1 Corinthians 3:16-17

> *In him the whole building is joined together and rises to become a holy temple in the Lord. And in him you too are being built together to become a dwelling in which God lives by his Spirit.* Ephesians 2:21-22

The Christian God is alive and active in all true followers of Jesus Christ. He is a personal God to them, abiding and living in their very being. What a contrast to the sterile and impotent gods of the Greeks, defined by earthly creatures in the form of idols! As Paul made his way through Athens and other cities in ancient Greece, he wanted to make it clear to all who would listen that God is not limited or confined in any way by physical temples. He is much greater than any dwelling on this earth.

God is self-sufficient and self-reliant

To the erudite scholars on Mars Hill, Paul affirms with clarity that his God is complete in Himself and does not require anything from His creation to embellish or enhance His stature:

> *And he is not served by human hands, as if he needed anything, because he himself gives all men life and breath and everything else.* Acts 17:25

God does not require humanity to exist for Him to be Who He is. On the contrary, we are the ones that need Him. In the Old Testament, the Psalmist dispelled any notion that God was dependent on us or any of our gifts:

> *I have no need of a bull from your stall or of goats from your pens, for every animal of the forest is mine, and the cattle on a thousand hills. I know every bird in the mountains, and the creatures of the field are mine. If I were hungry I would not tell you, for the world is mine, and all that is in it.* Psalm 50:9-12

He gave us life, not vice versa. Because God is distinct from His creation and existed long before man was created, He is not affected by our actions or lack thereof. God was already in existence, complete in Himself, when He created Adam and Eve. He chooses to have a relationship with His creation and use them in His plan because this is what He desires, not because He is compelled to do so by some outside force. Some Christians have the mistaken notion that God *needed* fellowship as the reason He created human beings. The truth is God did not create Adam and Eve because He needed anything from them. The Lord already enjoyed sweet fellowship and covenant relationship within the Trinity. He created Adam and Eve and placed His image upon them because He desired to have a relationship with His reflected creation. The same is true of us today. We serve a complete God Who never changes, never has a bad day, and never runs out of energy or ability to meet the needs of His creation. Because of His completeness, we can draw from His fullness.

God is the intelligent Creator of mankind

To further add to the idea that God is close and interested in this world, Paul introduces the idea that he not only created the universe, He also created mankind.

> *From one man he made every nation of men that they should inhabit the whole earth; and he determined the times set for them and the exact places where they should live.* Acts 17:26

In this statement, Paul left no doubt that human beings are the result of God's creation and He is personally interested in them. The human race ultimately goes back to the creation of Adam. The debate over whether man is the handiwork of Almighty God rages in our culture today, as non-theistic forces, particularly in the scientific arena, find this idea untenable and irrational. Not so long ago in our country, the idea that human beings were created by God was commonly accepted as a fact. Today however, with the steady drumbeat of classical Darwinian evolution hammering our school systems with a non-theistic view of human origin, this idea of man as a unique creation of God is becoming less and less accepted. However, according to the Bible, in the beginning mankind occupied a special place in relationship to God because He created the human race in His image and likeness. Adam was to literally be the reflection of God:

> *Then God said, "Let us make man in our image, in our likeness, and let them rule over the fish of the sea and the birds of the air, over the livestock, over all the earth, and over all the creatures that move along the ground." So God created man in his own image, in the image of God he*

> *created him; male and female he created them.*
> Genesis 1:26-27

This was not true of any other animals. Thus the human race is placed in a very special and unique situation. The Hebrew words for *image* and *likeness* are *tselem* and *demuth*. The basic meaning in these words is to *reflect an image* or *resemble something in some way*. To be created in the image of God meant that the human race had qualities reflecting their Creator the animals did not have. These qualities included:

- Superior intellect
- Superior emotional responses
- Superior freedom of choice
- Superior self-consciousness
- Superior self-determination
- Super cognitive and logic skills
- Superior moral code
- Superior communication abilities
- Superior creative talents
- Superior spiritual consciousness

Because God is the Creator of man, humanity does have a frame of reference as to his origin, value and purpose in life. We discussed earlier the futility of living in a world devoid of God. Without a Creator who formed him, mankind has no real value, purpose or meaning. Francis Schaeffer poignantly reflects on what it means for mankind to be created in the image of God:

> *For Twentieth century man this phrase, the image of God, is as important as anything in Scripture, because men today can no longer answer that crucial question, "Who am I?" In his own naturalistic theories, with the uniformity of cause and effect in a closed system with an evolutionary concept of a mechanical chance parade from the atom to man, man has lost his unique identity.... In contrast, I stand in the flow of history. I know my origin. My lineage is longer than the Queen of England. It does not start with the battle of Hastings. It does not start with the beginnings of good families, wherever or whenever they lived. As I look at myself in the flow of space-time-reality, I see my origin in Adam and in God's creating man in His own image.* (Francis Schaeffer, *Genesis in Space and Time*, p.46)

God created mankind with purpose and meaning. We are made in His image. In Acts 17:26, Paul also declares that God has determined many parameters to guide humanity on this earth, such as geographical boundaries. We are not the products of random chance but of an intelligent Creator Who designated certain purposes for us. The human race can only find its true value, worth and purpose when it is in relationship with its Creator.

God is within our reach and desires that men seek Him

Previously, Paul addressed the Epicureans, who believed their gods were untouchable and remote. The Apostle declared to them that the true God is not distant or aloof but very knowable. Now, Paul is strategically targeting the Stoics who, in a pantheistic sense, already believed in the nearness of the "gods", with the idea that we can reach out to God and find Him:

> *God did this so that men would seek him and perhaps reach out for him and find him, though he is not far from each one of us.* Acts 17:27

Paul's idea of the "nearness" of God would have been different than the Stoics pantheistic sense of this. However, Paul does not hesitate to affirm that God is not far from us, and close enough that man can find and reach out to Him. Paul communicates God's desire to have a relationship with mankind and has made Himself known and accessible for this to happen.

The God of Christianity can be distinguished among the gods of other religions in that He desires to have a loving and affirming relationship with His creation. He is very accessible and available to all who would seek Him. There are two distinct concepts of God which are important to keep in mind when discussing our relationship to Him. One is called the "eminence" of God, whereby He is set apart and distinct from His creation. The extreme version of this is *deism*. The second is the "immanence" of God which defines Him as near and close to us. The extreme version of this is *pantheism*. This twofold dimension is unique to the God of Scripture. To have a bond with someone, we must have close proximity to them, yet they must be separate from us. The God of the Scripture is unique in that He desires to have a relationship with mankind and is nearer than we think. Even in the book of Genesis, the Bible depicts God as "walking in the garden in the cool of the day" to meet with Adam and Eve; something He apparently did often:

> *Then the man and his wife heard the sound of the LORD God as he was walking in the garden in the cool of the day, and they hid from the LORD God among the trees of the garden.* Genesis 3:8

To connect in a more meaningful way with the Stoic philosophers, Paul quotes from two of their own poets to reinforce his point:

> *For in him we live and move and have our being. As some of your own poets have said, "We are his offspring."* Acts 17:28

The first quotation, "For in him we live and move and have our being", is most likely from Epemenides the Cretan. The second, "We are his offspring" is from the poem *Natural Phenomena* by Aratus of Cilicia. Paul is clever to use cultural works familiar to his audience to reinforce his point on the relational aspect of God with His creation. This is a strategic tactic Christians should use with their audience. Sometimes it can be effective to allude to secular references from books, movies, music and pop culture to reinforce the spiritual points we are making to our audience. By quoting the Stoic poet, Paul is not intending to reinforce pantheism. Instead, he desires to bring a Christian perspective to illustrate the fact that the God Who created us is near and desires for us to know Him. This a relevant message for our generation as well.

God is invisible and cannot be replicated

There were many idols and replicas of gods in the ancient world of Greece, clearly visible to all who walked the streets of her ancient cities. These idols were reflected in numerous physical images forged by skilled craftsman that reflected all aspects of life from nature to love to fertility. Worshippers paid them homage, and performed many rituals of obeisance to appease them. By defining their gods in the forms of earthly images, the Greeks were placing limitations on them. This is why they had numerous gods to cover all the aspects of their world and lifestyle.

From the time that Cain presented an offering to God made from his own hands (Genesis 4:3), human beings have demonstrated a propensity for idol worship in the form of graven images crafted from their own abilities. Paul addresses this subject on Mars Hill:

> *Therefore since we are God's offspring, we should not think that the divine being is like gold or silver or stone—an image made by man's design and skill.* Acts 17:29

Many civilizations fashion idols in attempting to depict what their gods look like. All over the world, in every religious culture, one can find a motley display of physical manifestations of idols. The Lord made it clear in the Ten Commandments that He would not tolerate idolatry in any physical form:

> *You shall have no other gods before me. You shall not make for yourself an idol in the form of anything in heaven above or on the earth beneath or in the waters below. You shall not bow down to them or worship them; for I, the LORD your God, am a jealous God.* Exodus 20:3-5

In the Old Testament, the crafting and worship of idols was clearly forbidden:

> *All who make idols are nothing, and the things they treasure are worthless. Those who would speak up for them are blind; they are ignorant, to their own shame. Who shapes a god and casts an idol, which can profit him nothing? He and his kind will be put to shame; craftsmen are nothing but men. Let them all come together and take their stand; they will be brought down to terror and infamy.* Isaiah 44:9-11

Paul points out to the philosophers in Athens that God is invisible and cannot be defined by works of art or by man's creative abilities. He is proclaiming there is one invisible God in contrast to the many physical deities of the Greeks. Later in his letter to Timothy, the Apostle reaffirms that God is invisible:

> *Now to the King eternal, immortal, invisible, the only God, be honor and glory forever and ever. Amen.* 1 Timothy 1:17

The Apostle John records Jesus' words that God is "spirit", reinforcing His invisibility:

> *God is spirit, and his worshipers must worship in spirit and in truth.* John 4:24

God is much greater and more powerful than any created idol of man. Paul admonished the Corinthians Christians, many who had come out of idol worship, to flee from this type of religious participation. Worship of the true God is incompatible with the worship of any created idol:

> *Therefore, my dear friends, flee from idolatry.... Do I mean then that a sacrifice offered to an idol is anything, or that an idol is anything? No, but the sacrifices of pagans are offered to demons, not to God, and I do not want you to be participants with demons. You cannot drink the cup of the Lord and the cup of demons too; you cannot have a part in both the Lord's Table and the table of demons.* 1 Corinthians 10:14, 19-21

There are many replacement idols for the true Living God in our world. They do not always have to be made out of physical materials. They can take the form of money, status, and power. The message for our time is that there is only one true God, Who is boundless and limitless, and any substitute in the form of an idol will never fully satisfy.

God is merciful and commands repentance

In communicating the nature of God to those on Mars Hill, Paul's intention was for these Greek philosophers to understand that God was merciful and benevolent, desiring for man to repent of their wayward and sinful ways:

> *In the past God overlooked such ignorance, but now he commands all people everywhere to repent.* Acts 17:30

In stating that God overlooked such ignorance, Paul had to subtly be alluding to the "altar of the unknown god" he had encountered earlier during his walk through Athens. Perhaps, the Athenians were justified in expressing their ignorance of God, but Paul is now declaring there is no longer any excuse to be ignorant of the true and Living God, because he was introducing and defining Him in their midst. The philosophers needed to know that God truly desired for men to repent from their sin and was giving them the chance to do so. The implication here is that man is flawed, in need of repentance. Too many times, skeptics of Christianity only point to those places in the Bible that depict the Lord as angry and vengeful toward humanity and its sin, painting a portrait of Him as an ogre Who relishes in dispensing judgment on His creation. Paul speaks to this very clearly on Mars Hill in the verse referenced above by communicating that God is merciful in giving mankind a chance to repent.

In spite of all the evil in the world and mankind's resistance and hostility to the living God, Jehovah continues to beckon man to come to Him and receive forgiveness. The Living God truly loves the people of this planet, in spite of their sin and wickedness. He is a God of mercy and grace Who desires all men to repent and find Him. Paul and Peter both affirm God's penchant toward forgiveness in their epistles:

> *This is good, and pleases God our Savior, who wants all men to be saved and to come to a knowledge of the truth.* 1 Timothy 2:3-4

> *The Lord is not slow in keeping his promise, as some understand slowness. He is patient with you, not wanting anyone to perish, but everyone to come to repentance.* 2 Peter 3:9

God is a just judge and will bring history to an end
Paul make it clear to these scholars that, although God is merciful and loving toward His creation, one day He will judge the world with justice:

> *For he has set a day when he will judge the world with justice....* Acts 17:31

Christian theology maintains that the world is inexorably moving toward the end, which includes final judgment. This establishes the fact that there is a heaven and hell at the end of life's journey. The erroneous fantasy that all religion, regardless of what form it takes, will eventually lead to a blissful and harmonious future is debunked by Paul.

There exists much confusion regarding the judgment of God, even among many believers. I have heard Christians and pastors teach that God is judging the United States because of her wickedness and ungodliness. Recently, a well-meaning Christian friend related to me that his church was teaching that the recent spate of tragedies which had befallen the United States were the direct result of God's judgment because of America's sins. Using this logic, God would be remiss by not judging the whole world right now since all of mankind is sinful. We must be careful about making cavalier pronouncements about what and whom we think God is judging. Paul makes it clear in unequivocal terms that there will come a day in the future when God will judge the world, but that day has yet to arrive. This idea of a "day" of future judgment is also consistent with other teachings of the New Testament:

> *I tell you the truth, it will be more bearable for Sodom and Gomorrah on the day of judgment than for that town.* Matthew 10:15

> *But I tell you that men will have to give account on the day of judgment for every careless word they have spoken.* Matthew 12:36

Based on Paul's proclamation on Mars Hill, it is important for us to recognize that our salient message to the world today is for man to repent while there is still time, before final judgment ensues. I am not saying that God cannot exert punishment on individuals or nations if He so desires. But the world we are trying to reach needs to hear the message of hope that there is still time to find God in Christ before He does finally execute judgement on the world. This is a message much more consistent and compatible with what Paul declared on Mars Hill.

It is also important to note in Acts 17:31 that Paul reveals God will judge the world with justice. In other words, in His judgment, God is totally fair and right in everything He does. He is a totally righteous judge. The Old Testament affirms this as well:

> *But, O LORD Almighty, you who judge righteously and test the heart and mind, let me see your vengeance upon them, for to you I have committed my cause.* Jeremiah 11:20

When it comes to the final judgment, God cannot make mistakes. Each person who stands before Him in final judgment will be dispensed justice based on the integrity of God, the great and righteous Judge. His mercy will not last forever. History is inevitably moving toward a final conclusion. The Bible is unequivocal that eternal judgment awaits all those outside of Christ:

> *If anyone's name was not found written in the book of life, he was thrown into the lake of fire.* Revelation 20:15

God administers His plans through the resurrected Christ

Paul, in his final point to the philosophers on Mars Hill, now comes to the lynch pin of his argument: God will be active in this world through the resurrected Christ, the Man He has appointed to judge the world.

> *...by the man he has appointed. He has given proof of this to all men by raising him from the dead.* Acts 17:31

Jesus' declaration corroborates this statement by Paul:

> *Moreover, the Father judges no one, but has entrusted all judgment to the Son.* John 5:22

Ultimately, the clearest revelation about the nature of God is be found in the resurrected Christ. All of God's activity in the Old Testament, from Genesis to Malachi, was pointing to the coming of Jesus Christ: the God-man. God's involvement in the world is in conjunction with the Son of God, Who walked this earth, was crucified in history, and bodily rose from the dead. In essence, the work of God is verified in the person of Christ. Paul does not directly mention Christ's name but he had spoken of Christ and the resurrection in the market-place, where it is clear to Whom he was referencing (Acts 17:18). The Greeks worshiped an unknown god: one that couldn't be verified or defined. The Christian God was clearly defined and represented in the person of Jesus Christ:

To prove this man, Jesus, was worthy to be God's appointed representative to carry out His plans, Paul offers the credential of His resurrection from the dead. The translation *given proof* is made up of two Greek words: *parechō* which means *to offer* or *furnish*, and *pistis*, which is normally translated *faith* but here coveys the idea of a *conviction, confidence* or *proof*. The basis of this proof or evidence of Christ's authority is His resurrection from the dead. Bruce indicates this teaching on the resurrection would not have been widely accepted by most of Paul's audience:

> *The Greek attitude to resurrection is well expressed by the words which Aeschylus ascribes to Apollo on the very occasion when the court of the Areopagus was founded: "Once a man dies and the earth drinks up his blood, there is no resurrection" (the word is anastasis, the word so constantly on Paul's lips.* (F.F. Bruce, *Defence of the Gospel*, p. 47)

This cannot be emphasized enough - the resurrection of Jesus is the cornerstone of the Christian faith. It separates Christ apart from all others and certainly emboldened the early proclaimers of the faith, including Paul, to preach the gospel of Christ with reckless abandon, even at the expense of their lives. The One Who was judged by Pilate and condemned by the Jewish high council, will one day be the One to exercise judgment on the world.

Paul's Message Resonated with Some

The teaching of the resurrection of Christ had to be shocking to these scholars who, in their philosophical world, would find such an idea foreign, preposterous and untenable. The reaction to this astonishing and unique teaching on the resurrection caused some to scoff but others, who attended the seminar on Mars Hill, came to believe in the resurrected Christ.

> *When they heard about the resurrection of the dead, some of them sneered, but others said, "We want to hear you again on this subject." At that, Paul left the Council. A few men became followers of Paul and believed. Among them was Dionysius, a member of the Areopagus, also a woman named Damaris, and a number of others.* Acts 17:32-34

The lessons from Paul's lecture on Mars Hill are very relevant to us in the modern world in which we live. The God of Paul is verifiable, knowable and relational. His works and actions are woven into the fabric of history and human experience, chronicled in the Word of God.

His handiwork of creation is painted in the skies and the stars every night for the whole world to see. God is here. The earth and all of creation proclaim that He lives. He is also the creator of humanity and has endowed them with purpose and meaning. God calls mankind to repent from their rejection of Him. He manifested Himself through the person and work of Jesus Christ, a fact authenticated by His historical resurrection from the dead. Through Christ, God will one day judge the world. In contrast to the thousands of Greek gods, some defined and some not, there is only one true God and one true Savior.

On Mars Hill, Paul furnishes a template on how to communicate the living God of hope to a skeptical and hostile audience, as well as a religious culture whose views are often diametrically opposed to the Christian doctrine. We would be wise to use Paul's model in communicating the Living God to skeptics in our own day.

CHAPTER 8

GOOD GOD VS. EVIL WORLD

No discussion about God would be complete without discussing the issue of evil's existence. In defending our faith, we are often asked to explain the contradiction between a *good God* and an *evil world* that is full of pain and suffering. It is obvious to even the most obtuse observer that many things are wrong with our planet. Destructive forces operate all over the world and mankind does not know how to explain or deal with it. It is beyond our ability to make sense of genocide, murder, terrorism, as well as famine, disease, and devastating natural disasters. What makes matters worse is that nature's calamities are often directly blamed on God. Insurance companies have been known to designate natural disasters in their policy jargon as "acts of God." In a world that we call "God's world", it seems incongruous to harmonize a wicked planet with a good God. With this backdrop, it is understandable why much of humanity will not commit to the God of Christianity, Whom they believe ignores the plight of millions of innocent and helpless people.

The presence of evil cannot be entirely understood or explained, but it can be framed and given a perspective. Even the non-Christian and the atheist have a hard time explaining the origin of evil. Jesus entered into a world full of pain, sorrow and injustice. He did much to relieve the anguish of His generation but did not eradicate all sickness, hardship, injustice and suffering. Christianity is the only religion that offers a plausible explanation for the origin and existence of evil, as well as the antidote for it. There is no incompatibility between a good and loving God and the existence of an evil and destructive planet. John Warwick Montgomery, discusses this issue by proposing a series of questions that focuses on the ultimate question: "Why does God allow evil in the world?" (John Warwick Montgomery, *Sensible Christianity-Tape Series, Vol 1-3*) I have added an addition question as well.

Question 1: Is the Biblical View of God Inconsistent with Evil?

Answer: No. God did not cause or originate evil in the first place. The existence of evil is the responsibility of the creature, not the Creator. The Bible is clear that when God created the world it was good, devoid of imperfection and blemish. He did not bring sin and destruction into our planet, mankind did, as these Scriptures illustrate:

> *God saw all that he had made, and it was very good. And there was evening, and there was morning—the sixth day.* Genesis 1:31

> *Therefore, just as sin entered the world through one man, and death through sin, and in this way death came to all men, because all sinned.* Romans 5:12

God did not introduce sin and its destructive consequences into our world. It came through the man Adam. One of Adam's chief responsibilities as a mediator between his Creator and the earth was to keep evil out of it. He failed the test, consequently, his sin and disobedience not only brought destructive effects upon humanity, but the entire planet. God places the culpability for the pain and suffering of the earth squarely at the feet of Adam:

> *To Adam he said, "Because you listened to your wife and ate from the tree about which I commanded you, 'You must not eat of it,' cursed is the ground because of you; through painful toil you will eat of it all the days of your life."* Genesis 3:17

> *For the creation was subjected to frustration, not by its own choice, but by the will of the one who subjected it, in hope that the creation itself will be liberated from its bondage to decay and brought into the glorious freedom of the children of God. We know that the whole creation has been groaning as in the pains of childbirth right up to the present time.* Romans 8:20-22

Evil is not eternal. It had a beginning and, one day when Jesus returns, it will have an end. However, the existence of evil, necessitates that there also be a force of good as well.

Question 2: If God Did not Cause Evil, Why Did He Allow the Creature to Cause It?

Answer: The nature of God (love) must allow free will. God established His relationship with Adam and Eve on the basis of freedom of choice. He did not desire to fellowship and communicate with robots or mindless puppets. The Creator preferred that human beings choose to love Him, and gave them the option to do so. True love cannot exist without the option of the choice not to love. Love and the possibility of rejection always go hand-in-hand. For God to have proceeded in any other way would have produced automatons, not moral human beings. For the Lord to have made it impossible for Adam and Eve to fail would have made a mockery of love and relationships.

We understand this principle on the natural level. When we ask our children to do something or to abide by a certain rule in the house, we are aware that there is the possibility of them choosing not to do what we ask. If we followed them around every moment to prevent them from ever disobeying us, it would make a farce of the parenting relationship. Our desire is that our children would voluntarily, out of respect and love for us as parents, do what we ask but there is always the possibility they will not, and negative results may ensue. God gave Adam a clear cut directive and warned him of the dire consequences should he disobey:

> *And the LORD God commanded the man, "You are free to eat from any tree in the garden; but you must not eat from the tree of the knowledge of good and evil, for when you eat of it you will surely die."* Genesis 2:16-17

When Adam and Eve opted to rebel against their Creator and chose to go their own way by eating from the forbidden tree, evil entered the world and the commensurate pain and suffering that came with it. This was the consequence of choice, the fruit of rebellion and independence from God. For God not to have allowed the consequences would have made a sham of their relationship. He was compelled to do what He said would happen or else be a liar. Paul speaks of mankind's propensity to turn away from God when they knew Him and thus, He will allow them to suffer the consequences of their rebellion.

> *For since the creation of the world God's invisible qualities—his eternal power and divine nature—have been clearly seen, being understood from what has been made, so that men are without excuse. For although they knew God, they neither glorified him as God nor gave thanks to him, but their thinking became futile and their foolish hearts were darkened. Although they claimed to be wise, they became fools and exchanged the glory of the immortal God for images made to look like mortal man and birds and animals and reptiles. Therefore God gave them over in the sinful desires of their hearts to sexual impurity for the degrading of their bodies with one another.* Romans 1:20-24

Some will ask, "Since God knows everything, even what lies ahead in the future, explain why He didn't stop Adam from sinning since He knew beforehand that Adam would fail." The answer is simple: to do so would have interfered with the free choice of the humans. The relationship between God and Adam and Eve had to be based on only their choice to love and obey their Creator, not on a meddling, controlling and manipulating God. C.S. Lewis stated it well, "There are only two kinds of people; those who say to God, 'Thy will be done', and those to whom God says, 'All right, then, have it your way.'" (C.S. Lewis, *The Great Divorce,* p. 75)

Question 3: Why Does God Allow the Effects of Evil?

There are two answers to this question:

 # 1: We cannot eliminate the effects of our poor choices. If we remove consequences, we eviscerate the power of free will. Consequences go hand in hand with choices. Not to allow the effects of choice would have rendered senseless the whole process. What motivation is there to make good and moral decisions, if the consequences do not matter? If someone robs a bank knowing full well no punishment will ever happen to him if caught, he will be emboldened to keep robbing more banks. For God not to punish the disobedience of Adam and Eve would have made Him a liar. He would have promised one thing and not carried out what He said. The Bible makes it clear that we sow what we reap. There has to be negative ramifications and consequences for our poor decisions, even if they are painful:

> *He who sows wickedness reaps trouble, and the rod of his fury will be destroyed.* Proverbs 22:8

> *Do not be deceived: God cannot be mocked. A man reaps what he sows. The one who sows to please his sinful nature, from that nature will*

> *reap destruction; the one who sows to please the Spirit, from the Spirit will reap eternal life.* Galatians 6:7-8

 # 2: The second answer to the aforementioned question is that Satan is the god of this age (2 Corinthians 4:4) and many evil aspects in our world come directly from the satanic kingdom and his hierarchy of evil assistants. Although he is not more powerful than God, Satan does have limited authority to impact this world in an evil way. There is a devil who exists and inflicts great damage and pain on the lives of those who live on this earth. After healing the crippled woman on the Sabbath, Jesus indicates that her illness was in conjunction with the work of Satan (Luke 13:10-16). Matthew, in his gospel, records an incident where Jesus, after healing a blind and mute man, attributes his maladies to demon possession. Jesus later indicates that the man's healing was a direct result of Jesus casting out the demon (Matthew 12:22-28). There are a number of individuals on this planet who serve the evil one and carry out his destructive orders.

Years ago, while watching Billy Graham deliver the memorial message at the service for those killed in the Oklahoma City bombing, I was struck by how he dealt with evil in our world. He was honest about evil's mystery and admitted that he had even asked questions himself about why God allows hideous events like the bombing to occur. But his words were instructive and powerful as he tried to make some sense of the tragedy that had befallen Oklahoma City. He declared, "There is something about evil we will never understand this side of eternity. The Bible says two other things we are tempted to forget. It tell us there is a devil and that Satan is very real and has great power. It also tell us that evil is real and that the human heart is capable of almost limitless evil when it is cut off from God and the moral law." (from YouTube posting of Billy Graham's speech of April 23, 1995).

When Adam sinned, he opened the door for Satan to have limited authority on the earth. This authority is acutely manifested in those who reject the Living God as a force in their lives. Some people are shocked when I tell them there are two "gods" operating in our world. One is Jehovah, the God of Scripture. The second is Satan, better known as the devil. The Bible ascribes the title "god" to him and cedes the fact that he oversees a dominion of darkness from which followers of Christ have been delivered:

> *The god of this age has blinded the minds of unbelievers, so that they cannot see the light of the gospel of the glory of Christ, who is the image of God.* 2 Corinthians 4:4

> *For he has rescued us from the dominion of darkness and brought us into the kingdom of the Son he loves.* Colossians 1:13

The Bible also declares that Satan's work on earth is also abetted by human beings he influences and controls. At one time all of us who were outside of Christ fit into this category:

> *You belong to your father, the devil, and you want to carry out your father's desire. He was a murderer from the beginning, not holding to the truth, for there is no truth in him. When he lies,*

> *he speaks his native language, for he is a liar and the father of lies.* John 8:44

> *As for you, you were dead in your transgressions and sins, in which you used to live when you followed the ways of this world and of the ruler of the kingdom of the air, the spirit who is now at work in those who are disobedient.* Ephesians 2:1-2

> *We know that we are children of God, and that the whole world is under the control of the evil one.* 1 John 5:19

Certainly, nefarious names like Hitler, Stalin, Mao Tsetung, Idi Amin, and many others like them, remind us there are ruthless people inflicting great pain and suffering on our world. They are ultimately emissaries of Satan.

Question 4: Why Does God Allow So Many Effects of Evil?

Answer: Sometimes when the question is asked, "Why is the world so evil and why is there so much pain, suffering and injustice in it?" It would be helpful to answer this question with another question: "Why, with such a powerful evil force of Satan and so many wicked people in this world, do we see so much good around us?" The answer lies in the fact that God does limit the effects of evil. He does this in three primary ways:

1. **Through structures of society**
Evil can be curtailed and limited to some degree through the avenues and structures of society in our world which God has established as a deterrent to lawlessness and sinfulness. These structures include the family, economics, education and the political order. The Bible declares that the main role of government is to punish evil doers:

Everyone must submit himself to the governing authorities, for there is no authority except that which God has established. The authorities that exist have been established by God. Consequently, he who rebels against the authority is rebelling against what God has instituted, and those who do so will bring judgment on themselves. For rulers hold no terror for those who do right, but for those who do wrong. Do you want to be free from fear of the one in authority? Then do what is right and he will commend you. For he is God's servant to do you good. But if you do wrong, be afraid, for he does not bear the sword for nothing. He is God's servant, an agent of wrath to bring punishment on the wrongdoer. Romans 13:1-4

This Scripture ascribes the title of "God's servant" to governments in their role of punishing wickedness and evil. Other institutions such as the family unit, the work place, and educational systems also contribute to the decline of evil and sinful practices in a given region.

2. **Through Jesus Christ and His followers**
Jesus demonstrated a great ability to deal with evil, suffering and injustice while He walked the earth. When He announced the inauguration of His ministry at the synagogue in Nazareth, recorded in the book of Luke, He stated that one of the purposes of His ministry was to help alleviate the suffering and destitute situations existing at that time:

The Spirit of the Lord is on me, because he has anointed me to preach good news to the poor. He has sent me to proclaim freedom for the prisoners and recovery of sight for the blind, to release the oppressed, to proclaim the year of the Lord's favor. Luke 4:18-19

Now, He has forwarded this ministry on to His followers to carry out His life and message for as long as His final coming is delayed. Both the teachings and practices of our Lord were designed to curtail the kingdom of darkness. If the church were removed from this planet, people on this earth would destroy each other because of the unbridled wickedness and evil that would take over. Jesus stressed in His message to Peter, the overcoming powerful nature of the church against the "gates of Hades" and the forces of evil:

And I tell you that you are Peter, and on this rock I will build my church, and the gates of Hades will not overcome it. I will give you the keys of the kingdom of heaven; whatever you bind on earth will be bound in heaven, and whatever you loose on earth will be loosed in heaven. Matthew 16:18-19

As long as the church is on earth, there will be a force to face, confront, and limit evil in this world.

3. **Through Jesus' final return**
   Evil, suffering and pain will never be totally eradicated from this planet until Jesus returns. Christian theology is a belief system that offers hope for today but looks forward to the future when one day, Christ will return and rid this world of all aspects of suffering and pain. Satan, along with his minions and helpers, will one day be destroyed and a new heaven and earth will be established, reversing all negative results of the original fall of Adam and Eve in the Garden of Eden. At the end of the book of Revelation, John writes that one day, after the return of Christ, there will be no more tears or pain and all things will be made new:

   Then I saw a new heaven and a new earth, for the first heaven and the first earth had passed away, and there was no longer any sea. I saw the Holy City, the new Jerusalem, coming down out of heaven from God, prepared as a bride beautifully dressed for her husband. And I heard a loud voice from the throne saying, "Now the dwelling of God is with men, and he will live with them. They will be his people, and God himself will be with them and be their God. He will wipe every tear from their eyes. There will be no more death or mourning or crying or pain, for the old order of things has passed away" He who

> *was seated on the throne said, "I am making everything new!" Then he said, "Write this down, for these words are trustworthy and true."* Revelation 21:1-5

Question 5—Does Evil Play a Valuable Role in the World?

Answer: Yes, it does. It can appear contradictory and incongruous with our sense of fairness to assign any positive attribute toward the existence of evil, suffering and pain. However, in an ironic way, evil and suffering can provide many useful purposes. Certainly the Bible recognizes value in suffering and pain. Here are some potential benefits:

1. Pain and suffering continually remind us that we live in an evil and imperfect world and highlights our vulnerability to that world. It is this pain that should lead mankind to embrace a healing and loving God. Normally, it is not during the good times when individuals seek God but in times of distress and pain. Pain and suffering continually remind us of the limitations and temporal nature of this fallen and flawed planet, and should cause us to seek hope in the Creator and long for our eternal home. In biblical times, many came to Jesus because of their helpless and hopeless situation. They found in Him answers for their pain and issues that could only be found in God. We normally don't seek the services of a doctor unless we are ill, the same can also be said of God.

2. Pain and suffering allow God to perform His miracles among us for His glory. It was to a deeply distressed world that Jesus came and, in the midst of the chaos, demonstrated the very power of the kingdom of God. Jesus could have eradicated all semblance of injustice and distress but chose not to. He has left a job for His church to do. We are carrying on the healing and restoring power of Christ in the world today. The church is advancing the very same kingdom of power and deliverance that Jesus demonstrated (Matthew 16:16-18). This world of suffering and evil provides a giant stage for God to demonstrate His power and love.

3. Pain and suffering permit us to minister and share the love of God to each other in our difficulties. It is amazing to see individuals and communities come together in times of tragedy and heartache. Sometimes, the best of humanity is brought out in the worst of times, whether a devastating tornado or hurricane that ravages a city, or a deranged madman who mass murders in a theater or office place. These calamitous situations usher forth the "better angels" of humanity.

4. Pain and suffering test the integrity of our faith and commitment to God. It is one thing to serve God when life is good, it is another when life hurts. Jesus called His followers to potentially suffer persecution, hardship and even die for Him. Our fidelity and allegiance to the Lord will often be challenged in the difficulties of our lives. Hardly a day goes by when we are not made

aware that followers of Jesus Christ are being persecuted and killed by evil forces. James places this in perspective:

> *Consider it pure joy, my brothers, whenever you face trials of many kinds, because you know that the testing of your faith develops perseverance. Perseverance must finish its work so that you may be mature and complete, not lacking anything.* James 1:2-4

5. Pain and suffering continually remind us of the evil forces that exist on our planet and, at the same time, provide an arena in which Satan can be defeated and Jesus uplifted. Many times during His ministry, Christ entered the arena of suffering that Satan had created and defeated him (Matthew 12:22-28). Like Jesus, we are commissioned to preach good news to the oppressed and rescue those under the control of Satan today. The church is now advancing this same victory over the devil.

6. Pain and suffering can place us in a position to hear God when we might not otherwise listen to Him. In regards to this matter, C.S. Lewis has poignantly stated:

> *God whispers to us in our pleasures, speaks to our conscience, but shouts in our pains. It is His megaphone to rouse a deaf world.* (C.S. Lewis, *The Problem of Pain*, p. 25)

As long as there is imperfection and despair in this world, there will always be the opportunity for men to seek God.

The problem of evil and pain on our planet is a difficult issue with which to deal. Those things we do not understand we must, by faith, place in the hands of the Lord and leave it there. There are no easy explanations but God has gone out of His way to help mitigate the effects that Adam's fall brought to our earth and that which Satan perpetuates through the hearts of evil men. As Christian apologists, it is our responsibility to present to our generation a loving God Who is actively involved in lifting men out of their despair today and giving them hope for the future. Christianity is the only religion that can offer this assurance.

CHAPTER 9

ARE BIBLICAL DOCUMENTS RELIABLE?

Christian theology is based not only on a belief in the existence of God, but also on the premise that God revealed Himself in history, recorded in the pages of the Bible and in the person of Jesus Christ. God is, by nature, a communicator with His creation. Therefore, because of the role biblical documents play in the revelation of this God, it is essential that they be accurate and reliable.

Our goal is to encourage the non-Christian to verify matters related to Christianity as he would with any other event or narrative of history. This applies to the original biblical documents. It is important to investigate and explore the principles one would use to verify the credibility of historical documents and, more specifically, how these principles apply to biblical documents. We should not assume that the Bible is true if the objective standards used to verify the biblical documents would bring into question the veracity of the Scriptures. Such verification is one of the major factors that sets Christianity apart from other religions. We go out of our way to invite the skeptic to analyze and test the accuracy of our documents. John Warwick Montgomery astutely identifies three ways to verify a historical document, which can be applied to the biblical manuscripts (John Warwick Montgomery, *History and Christianity*).

Bibliographical Verification

Verifying a document by the bibliographical method examines the transmission path by which the text reaches us. In other words, since we do not possess the original documents and are hundreds of years removed from their original transmission, it is imperative to determine the reliability of the existing copies. To do this, it is important to examine the number of manuscripts in existence and the time interval between the original and the copies we have today. Obviously, the greater the time between the original document and its copies, the more likely the chance of error. Here are some bibliographical principles utilized which can be helpful in the defense of the biblical manuscripts.

There is an abundance of manuscripts

The original New Testament books were written in *Koine* Greek, the Greek of the common people. There are more than 5,000 Greek manuscript copies of portions of the New Testament available to us today. When one includes copies in Latin and other languages, that number exceeds 24,000. No other literary work in history has this much manuscript support still in existence. For example, Homer's *Iliad* was written in 900 BC, and the earliest copy we have is from 400 BC. This is a time span of 500 years and 643 copies are available. The abundance of New-Testament manuscripts available allows students of textual criticism (the study of written work that attempts to establish the original text) to piece together the original document with a great degree of accuracy.

Some manuscripts are dated very close to the first century

Manuscripts of the New Testament were generally written on papyrus paper. Each papyrus is designated by the letter p and a number. Some of the manuscripts were inscribed in capital letters and were called *uncials*, while others were written in lower-case letters and were referred to as *minuscules*. Here is a list of some of the earliest and most important manuscripts of the New Testament that attest to its authenticity.

The John Rylands Fragment - p52

This papyrus (2 1/2 by 31/2 inches) contains five verses from the book of John (18:31-33, 37-38) and is the earliest known copy of any portion of the New Testament. It is dated between 117 and 138 AD. Jack Finegan says of this fragment:

> *Paleographically, the way individual letters are formed has been compared most closely with papyri of the end of the first or beginning of the second century, among them one bearing dates corresponding to AD 94 and AD 127. It is probable, therefore, that the present papyrus also belongs at the end of the first or beginning of the second century, at all events hardly later than AD 125.* (Jack Finegan, *Encountering New Testament Manuscripts*, p. 86.)

The finding of this papyrus is extremely important. Metzger notes:

> *Just as Robinson Crusoe, seeing but a single footprint in the sand, concluded that another human being, with two feet, was present on the island with him, so p52 proves the existence and use of the Fourth Gospel during the first half of the second century in a provincial town along the Nile.... Had this little fragment been known during the middle of the past century, that school of New Testament criticism which was inspired by the brilliant Tübingen professor, Ferdinand Christian Baur, could not have argued that the Fourth Gospel was not composed until about the year 160.* (Bruce Metzger, *Text of the New Testament*, p. 39)

The Bodmer Papyri - p66, p72, p75

These manuscripts are dated around 200 AD. They contain most of the gospels of John and Luke along with the books of Jude and 1 and 2 Peter. The Bodmer manuscripts contain the earliest complete copies of New-Testament books.

The Chester Beatty Papyri - p46

This papyrus is dated about 200 AD and, according to Sir Fredric Kenyon, is one of the most important manuscripts ever discovered. This papyrus consists of eighty-six slightly mutilated leaves, which contains portions from ten of Paul's epistles. These epistles include Romans, 1 and 2 Corinthians, Ephesians, Galatians, Philippians, Colossians, 1 and 2 Thessalonians and Hebrews.

Codex Vaticanus - B

This uncial is located in the great Vatican Library of Rome, which has been its home since sometime prior to 1475. This manuscript is dated between 325 and 350 AD and contains almost the entire New Testament and is, perhaps, the oldest uncial on parchment.

Codex Sinaiticus - Aleph

This manuscript was discovered about the middle of the nineteenth century by Dr. Constantine von Tischendorf at the monastery of St. Catharine on Mount Sinai. It once contained the entire Bible but today parts of the Old Testament have perished. However, the entire New Testament has survived. This manuscript is dated about 350 AD.

Codex Ephraemi Rescriptus - C

This manuscript is dated around 450 AD and contains most of the New Testament.

Codex Alexandrinus - A

This papyrus dates from about 450 AD and comprises the Old Testament and most of the New Testament: a complete manuscript of the Bible.

These are but a sampling of the manuscript evidence available to support the reliability of the biblical documents we have today. Astonishingly, Geisler and Nix state that, because of the manuscript evidence available to scholars today, it is estimated we have an accurate copy of 99.5 percent of the original New-Testament documents:

> *The New Testament has about 20,000 lines; the Iliad about 15,600. Only 40 lines (or 400 words) of the New Testament are in doubt, whereas 764 lines of the Iliad are questioned. This 5 percent textual corruption compares with one-half of 1 percent of similar emendations in the New Testament.* (Norman Geisler & William Nix. *A General Introduction to the Bible*, pp. 366-367)

All of this means is that the New-Testament documents from the first century have been carefully preserved to provide us a very accurate record of what was originally written by the New-Testament writers.

The church fathers supported manuscript reliability

Another bibliographical aspect which lends credence to the manuscript reliability of the biblical documents is the abundance of material found in the writings of the church fathers. They quoted extensively from the Bible. The church fathers lived in the first and second centuries and some of them knew the original apostles. Harold Greenlee observes:

> *Quotations of the Scriptures in the works of the early Christian writers are so extensive that the New Testament could virtually be reconstructed from them without the use of the New Testament*

> *manuscripts.* (Harold Greenlee. *Introduction to New Testament Textual Criticism*, p. 54)

Here is a list of some of the early church fathers and their quotations from New- Testament manuscripts.

Clement of Rome (95 AD)
Appointed by Peter, he quoted extensively from eight New-Testament books.

Ignatius (70-110 AD)
Martyred when he was the Bishop of Antioch, he had quoted from fifteen New-Testament books.

Polycarp (70-156 AD)
Polycarp was a disciple of John, spoke profusely of the Scriptures and was martyred at the age of 86.

Clement of Alexandria (150-212 AD)
He made more than 2,400 quotations from all but three books of the New Testament.

Tertullian (160-220 AD)
He quotes the New Testament more than 7,000 times, of which 3,800 quotations are from the gospels.

Hillolytus (170-235 AD)
His writings contain more than 1,300 references to the New Testament.

Origen (185-254 AD)
He lists more than 18,000 New-Testament quotations in his 6,000 works.

When one adds up the number of quotations from the New Testament in writings prior to 325 AD, the total is between 32,000 and 35,000 references. This adds support to the accuracy of the New Testament

Note on Old-Testament manuscripts
More has been said about the New Testament than the Old Testament. The reason for this is since the New Testament chronicles the life and ministry of Christ as well as the foundation of the Christian church, it is more relevant for our purposes to focus on New-Testament documents. However, the finding of the Dead Sea Scrolls did much to substantiate the manuscripts of the Old Testament.

In 1947 a little shepherd boy discovered the Dead Sea Scrolls in the Qumran caves near the Dead Sea. They were written by a strict sect of the Jews called the Essenes, dating from the time of Christ. This religious group had broken away from the temple-centered worship at Jerusalem and established their own monastic and Messianic community in the Judean desert near Qumran. Scientific dating on many of the items found in the caves date these scrolls back to the century before Christ and the first century AD. This was an incredible discovery because, prior to 1947, the earliest manuscript we had of the Old Testament was from about 900 AD. However, one of the Dead Sea Scrolls found is a complete manuscript of the Hebrew text of the book of Isaiah, which was dated by paleontologists at around 125 BC. This computes to a difference of one thousand years. Gleason Archer states:

> *The two copies of Isaiah discovered in Qumran Cave proved to be word for word identical with our standard Hebrew Bible in more than 95% of the text.* (Gleason Archer, *A Survey of Old Testament Introduction*, p.19)

The Hebrew scribes were meticulous in their transmission of the Hebrew manuscripts. Again, the accuracy of the biblical manuscripts is astonishing.

External Verification

The first way to examine the accuracy of historical documents is through bibliographical evidence. Montgomery suggest the second way to test the accuracy of an historical document is by means of external sources. The question is asked, "Do sources outside of the Bible itself confirm its accuracy?" The answer is simply "yes".

Extra-biblical sources

An abundance of extra-biblical sources affirm the accuracy and authenticity of the Scriptures. Many church fathers and historians have commented on them.

Papias, the Bishop of Hierapaolis (130 AD)

Eusebius, in his *Ecclesiastical History*, preserved the writings of Papias, who had received instruction from the Apostle John. The following excerpts gives illumination between the relationship of Mark and Peter in the transmission of the Gospels.

> *The elder used to say this also: Mark, having been the interpreter of Peter, wrote down accurately all that he [Peter] mentioned, whether sayings or doings of Christ, not, however, in order. For he was neither a hearer nor a companion of the Lord; but afterwards, as I said, he accompanied Peter, who adapted his teachings as necessity required, not as though he were making a compilation of the sayings of the Lord. So then Mark made no mistake, writing down in this way some things as he [Peter] mentioned to them; for he paid attention to this one thing, not to omit anything that he had heard, not to include any false statement among them.* (Eusebius. *Ecclesiastical History*, p. 127)

Irenaeus, Bishop of Lyons (180 AD)

Irenaeus had been a disciple of the Apostle John and wrote concerning the viability of the Gospels:

> *So firm is the ground upon which these Gospels rest, that the very heretics themselves bear witness to them, and, starting from these [documents], each one of them endeavors to establish his own particular doctrine.* (Cited by Josh McDowell in *Evidence That Demands a Verdict*, p. 63)

Josephus, first-century Jewish historian

A great extra-biblical source, which substantiates the Bible's accuracy and reliability, is the work of Flavius Josephus. He was a first-century Jewish historian who validated much of the New Testament, including the person of Jesus Christ. Josephus also recorded the terrible siege of Jerusalem in 70 AD, supporting the predictions of the gospel writers. The Romans gave him press credentials so that he could witness firsthand the carnage during the invasion of Jerusalem.

His works, *Jewish Antiquities* and *The Jewish War,* shed much light on the years prior to the birth of Christ and confirm events, dates and key players in the incidents after the death of Christ (e.g., the conflict between the Roman Empire and the Jewish nation). Josephus' works are absolutely invaluable in affirming the New Testament's accuracy. Here is an excerpt from his writings confirming the death of John the Baptist and supporting the New-Testament account of this historical event:

> *Now some of the Jews thought that Herod's army had been destroyed by God, and that it was a very just penalty to avenge John, surnamed the Baptist. For Herod had killed him, though he was a good man, who bade the Jews practice virtue, be just one to another, and pious toward God, and come together in baptism.* (Flavius Josephus, cited from F.F. Bruce in, *The New Testament Documents: Are They Reliable?*, p. 106)

Archaeology

Another extra biblical source which verifies much of what is in the Bible is the study of archaeology. The Bible was not written in secret. It was chronicled out in the open for all to witness. It incorporates a voluminous amount of historical information, major civilizations, and geographical locations within the scope of its long narrative. The science of archaeology (the study of material remains of past cultures) has substantiated literally thousands of places, rulers, peoples, artifacts, and events mentioned in the biblical narrative. Hundreds of books are available today on the subject of biblical archaeology and, thanks to the persistent and meticulous endeavors of Jewish archaeologists and others like them, many more finds are occurring every year, further substantiating the truth of the Bible. Here is what some leading archaeologists have said about the accuracy of the Scriptures.

Nelson Glueck, renowned Jewish archaeologist, stated:

> *It may be stated categorically that no archaeological discovery has ever controverted a biblical reference.* (Nelson Glueck. *Rivers in the Desert,* p.31)

William F. Fullbright, known as one of the greatest archaeologists of our time, had this to say:

> *Discovery after discovery has established the accuracy of innumerable details, and has brought increased recognition to the value of the Bible as a source of history.* (William Fullbright. *The Archaeology of Palestine,* pp. 127-128.)

Sir William Ramsay, at one time, was an ardent skeptic regarding the accuracy of the Bible. He spent thirty years in research on Luke's writings and verified almost all of Paul's travels and historic references. His words are powerful:

> *But, while recognizing the risk, and the probable condemnation that awaits the rash attempt, I will venture to add one to the number of the critics, by stating in the following chapters reasons for placing the author of Acts among the historians of the first rank.* (Sir William Ramsay. *ST. PAUL the Traveller and the Roman Citizen*, p. 4)

There have been hundreds of archaeological discoveries over the last two hundred years that have literally authenticated much of the data and information recorded in the Scriptures. When one realizes the Bible was written by numerous diverse authors over hundreds of years, in many different cultures and nations, archaeological evidence provides a powerful support that the Bible is one of the most accurate books ever written.

Let's take a look at just a sampling of some of the important archaeological finds discovered over the years. Most of these were compiled by the *Christian Research Journal*, volume 27, number 2 (2004).

Flood epic

There have been numerous finds in ancient civilizations discussing a great cataclysmic flood which engulfed the earth. This supports Noah's flood narrative as discussed in the book of Genesis. However, none is more important than what was discovered in the Gilgamesh Epic. This is an epic poem from ancient Mesopotamia that is recognized as the earliest surviving great work of literature. The epic begins with five Sumerian poems about 'Bilgamesh' (Sumerian for Gilgamesh), king of Uruk, dating from the Third Dynasty of Ur around 2100 BC). This epic poem describes a great flood sent as punishment by the gods, with humanity saved only when the pious Utnapishtim (the Mesopotamian Noah) builds a ship and saves the animal world. Unger elucidates:

> *Of all the ancient traditions which bear upon the Old Testament, the Babylonian Flood story as incorporated in the Epic of Gilgamesh manifest the most striking and detailed similarity to the Bible. The Sumerian Noah, Ziusundra, appears in the Babylonian translation of his name as Utnapishtim, "Day of Life." The exciting adventures of Gilgamesh and his eventual search for eternal life bring him at length to Utnapishtim, the immortal. The latter, in explaining to Gilgamesh the manner in which he obtained immortality, gives a full account of the Deluge. It is this feature of the Epic of Gilgamesh together with the view it gives of the ancients' belief in life after death that gives it special interest to students of the bible.* (Merrill Unger, *Archaeology and the Old Testament*, pp. 49-50)

The tremendous amount of detail in this epic that parallels the Genesis account of the flood is striking. It demonstrates that the flood epic in Genesis was not a fantasy, but a real event that has found itself transmitted through the years in the writing of ancient peoples.

The existence of the Hittites

In Genesis 23, we are told that Abraham buried his wife Sarah in the Cave of Machpelah, which he purchased from Ephron the Hittite. In 1 Samuel 11, the story is told of David's adultery with Bathsheba, the wife of Uriah the Hittite. Until a century ago, the Hittites were not known outside of the Old Testament, leading to the speculation by critics of the Bible to claim that they never existed but were made up by the writer.

However, in 1906, east of Ankara, Turkey, archaeologists discovered the ruins of Hattusas, the ancient Hittite capital, as well as an array of Hittite historical records, which revealed an empire flourishing in the mid-second millennium BC. This is a time frame that dove tails with the life of Abraham.

Biblical cities attested archaeologically

Numerous biblical cities have been discovered through the science of archaeology. Places such as Haran, Hazor, Dan, Megiddo, Shechem, Samaria, Shiloh, Beth Shemesh, Caesarea Phillipi and Beersheba have all been verified as historical sites.

Also, the five cities of Israel's archenemy the Philistines (as mentioned in the Bible) have been excavated and confirmed as historical sites. They include Ashkelon, Ashdod, Gaza, Gath and Ekron. These cities are primarily coastal which fits the nature of the Philistines because they were a people of the sea.

Shishak's invasion of Judah

1 Kings 14 and 2 Chronicles 12 speak of Pharaoh Shishak's conquest of Judah in the fifth year of the reign of King Rehoboam, the son of Solomon. This victory is commemorated in hieroglyphic wall carvings on the Temple of Amon at Thebes.

The Moabite stone

In 2 Kings 3, we are introduced to Mesha, the king of Moab, who rebelled against the king of Israel (Omri) following the death of Ahab. A three-foot stone slab, called the Mesha Stele was discovered, confirming the revolt by claiming triumph over Ahab's family, c.850 BC, and that Israel had "perished forever."

Obelisk of Shalmaneser III

In 2 Kings 9-10, Jehu is mentioned as King of Israel (841-814 BC). Assyria was already placing pressure on the northern kings even before their ultimate conquest in 722 BC. This has been proven by a six-and-a-half foot black obelisk discovered in the ruins of the palace at Nimrud in 1846. On it, Jehu is shown kneeling before Shalmaneser III and offering tribute to the Assyrian king, the only relief we have to date of a Hebrew monarch.

Burial Plaque of King Uzziah

King Uzziah of Judah ruled from 792-740 BC. In 2 Chronicles 26, his sin is recorded, which resulted in his being struck with leprosy later in his life. When Uzziah died, he was interred in a "field of burial" that belonged to the kings. His stone burial plaque has been discovered on the Mount of Olives and it reads: "Here, the bones of Uzziah, King of Judah, were brought. Do not open."

Hezekiah's Siloam tunnel inscription

King Hezekiah of Judah ruled from 721 BC to 686 BC. Fearing a siege by the Assyrian King Sennacherib, Hezekiah preserved Jerusalem's water supply by cutting a tunnel through 1,750 feet of solid rock from the Gihon Spring to the Pool of Siloam inside the city walls (2 Kings 20:20; 2 Chronicles 32:3-4; Isaiah 22:9ff.). At the Siloam end of the tunnel, an inscription (presently in the archaeological museum at Istanbul, Turkey), celebrates this remarkable achievement. The tunnel is still functioning today and is one of the few biblical sites that has virtually remained unchanged for 2,700 years. I have seen this tunnel and pool and it is truly an amazing testimony to the accuracy of the Old- Testament Scriptures.

The Sennacherib prism

After conquering the ten northern tribes of Israel, the Assyrians turned their attention southward to do the same to Judah. These events are recorded in 2 Kings 18-19. The prophet Isaiah told King Hezekiah that God would protect Judah against Sennacherib's assault (2 Chronicles 23; Isaiah 36-37). This is exactly what happened when God virtually destroyed the army of the Assyrians in the process (2 Kings 19:35-37).

Archaeological finds have corroborated that Assyrian records confirm this event. The cuneiform on a hexagonal, 15-inch baked clay prism found at the Assyrian capital of Nineveh, describes Sennacherib's invasion of Judah in 701 BC in which it claims that the Assyrian king shut Hezekiah inside Jerusalem "like a caged bird". However, like the biblical record, it does not say that he conquered Jerusalem which the prism certainly would have done if that had been the case. Jerusalem would not fall until 586 BC to the Babylonians. The finding of this prism confirms the accuracy of the biblical record.

The cylinder of Cyrus the Great

We find recorded in 2 Chronicles 36:23 and Ezra 1 that Cyrus the Great of Persia, after conquering Babylon, permitted Jews living there in captivity to return to their land. This is also prophesied in Isaiah 44:28.

This edict is corroborated by the discovery of a nine-inch clay cylinder found at Babylon from the time of its conquest, 539 BC. It reports Cyrus's victory and the subsequent policy of permitting Babylonian captives to return to their homes and even rebuild the temple.

Jeremiah's two names

On a trip to Israel, while visiting the City of David, it was revealed to us that archaeologists had recently unearthed evidence authenticating the book of Jeremiah. An archaeological dig led by Professor Eilat Mazar of Jerusalem's

Hebrew University, uncovered an intact seal impression, or "bula" bearing the name *Gedaliahu ben Pashur*. The bula is actually a stamped engraving made of mortar. This bula was found a few meters away from the site where a second seal, belonging to *Yuchal ben Shlemiyahu* was found three years earlier at the entrance of the City of David.

What makes these finds so incredible is that both names are recorded in Jeremiah 38:1-4:

> *Shephatiah son of Mattan,* ***Gedaliah son of Pashhur, Jehucal son of Shelemiah****, and Pashhur son of Malkijah heard what Jeremiah was telling all the people when he said, "This is what the LORD says: 'Whoever stays in this city will die by the sword, famine or plague, but whoever goes over to the Babylonians will live. He will escape with his life; he will live.' And this is what the LORD says: 'This city will certainly be handed over to the army of the king of Babylon, who will capture it.'" Then the officials said to the king, "This man should be put to death. He is discouraging the soldiers who are left in this city, as well as all the people, by the things he is saying to them. This man is not seeking the good of these people but their ruin." "He is in your hands," King Zedekiah answered. "The king can do nothing to oppose you."* Jeremiah 38:1-5

These two men were ministers in King Zedekiah's government, who reigned from 597-586 BC. They demanded the death penalty for the prophet Jeremiah after he pleaded for the king to surrender the city to King Nebuchadnezzar. Jeremiah's life was spared but his prophecy rang true. In

586 BC, Nebuchadnezzar destroyed the temple and ravaged the city of Jerusalem. The engraving of these names lay preserved for 2600 years and absolutely support the reliability of the Old-Testament documents. (Information provided in an article written by Hana Levi Julian in Arutz Sheva (Israel National News), August 03, 2008.)

These highlights of archaeological discoveries are only the tip of a mountain of archaeological evidence produced over hundreds of years and represent only a portion of the hundreds of archaeological discoveries supporting the accuracy of the biblical documents we hold dear.

Internal Verification

Montgomery suggests the third way the reliability of a document can be affirmed is through internal observations. This method revolves around and relates to the integrity of the authors. Questions are raised such as: "Were they close to the original event?", "What was their character?", "Is there evidence they were honest and factual in reporting?". These factors are important because we are dealing with first-century authors who claimed to be eyewitnesses of everything Jesus said and did. If it can be substantiated that they are honest and reliable sources of information, we have reason to trust their writings. For instance, a man who wrote about Abraham Lincoln in 1860 should be a more reliable source than someone writing about Mr. Lincoln in 1960. Typically, the closer the author is to the original event he is describing, the more trustworthy we expect him to be. All evidence available corroborates the idea that the New Testament is a product of first-century witnesses who were accurate and reliable in their reporting.

New-Testament authors were contemporaries of Jesus Christ

The New-Testament writers were either close companions of Jesus and direct eyewitnesses of Jesus activities, or were close associates with the original disciples. Luke, who falls into the latter category, commences his gospel by defending his meticulous research and reliance on first-hand witnesses to pen his book for the purpose of presenting an accurate account of the life of Christ:

> *Many have undertaken to draw up an account of the things that have been fulfilled among us, just as they were handed down to us by those who from the first were eyewitnesses and servants of the word. Therefore, since I myself have carefully investigated everything from the beginning, it seemed good also to me to write an orderly account for you, most excellent Theophilus, so that you may know the certainty of the things you have been taught.* Luke 1:1-4

The Apostle Peter goes out of his way to dispel any notion that what he wrote in his epistle was some cooked up story or fairy tale but was genuinely a firsthand accounting of what he saw:

> *We did not follow cleverly invented stories when we told you about the power and coming of our Lord Jesus Christ, but we were eyewitnesses of his majesty.* 2 Peter 1:16

John is even more vivid in the defense of his writings, as he appeals to the up front and close nature of his witness to the life of Christ, particularly the crucifixion:

> *That which was from the beginning, which we have heard, which we have seen with our eyes, which we have looked at and our hands have touched—this we proclaim concerning the Word of life. The life appeared; we have seen it and testify to it, and we proclaim to you the eternal life, which was with the Father and has appeared to us. We proclaim to you what we have seen and heard, so that you also may have fellowship with us. And our fellowship is with the Father and with his Son, Jesus Christ.* 1 John 1:1-3

> *But when they came to Jesus and found that he was already dead, they did not break his legs. Instead, one of the soldiers pierced Jesus' side with a spear, bringing a sudden flow of blood and water. The man who saw it has given testimony, and his testimony is true. He knows that he tells the truth, and he testifies so that you also may believe.* John 19:33-35

We know that these disciples of Jesus were, for the most part, independent of each other. Jesus appeared to them at least ten times during the 40 days after His resurrection (Acts 1:3). Most of the disciples were initially inclined to disbelieve what had happened to Him (John 20:25). Jesus showed them tangible evidence of His resurrection by eating with them, showing Thomas His scarred hands and feet, and demonstrating with many proofs that He was indeed alive (Acts 1:3). Furthermore, the accounts of the life of Christ are quite divergent and highlight different details that give us a complete picture of His story. Luke and Paul, though not original apostles, were contemporaries of the apostles and knew them well. Paul had direct encounters with Christ which started on the Damascus road and continued throughout his life, (2 Corinthians 12:7-8). Everything we know about these men indicates that they were honest, full of integrity, and believed in Christ even to the point of death. There is nothing to suggest they were insane, inept, or given to hallucination.

All New-Testament documents are first-century manuscripts

New-Testament documents were written in the first century and were composed very close to the time of Jesus and Paul. Scholar F.F. Bruce states:

> *The New Testament was complete, or substantially complete, about AD 100, the majority of the writing being in existence twenty to forty years before this.... At any rate, the time elapsing between the evangelic events and the writing of most of the New Testament books, was, from the standpoint of historical research satisfactorily short. For in assessing the trustworthiness of ancient historical writings, one of the most important questions is: How soon after the events took place were they recorded?* (F.F. Bruce, *The New Testament Documents*, p. 14)

Dr. William Fullbright, the eminent archaeologist from Johns Hopkins University, endorses the conclusion that the New-Testaments documents were first-century compositions:

> *We can already and emphatically say that there is no longer any solid basis for dating any book of the New Testament after about 80 AD. Every book of the New Testament was written by a baptized Jew between the forties and the eighties of the first century....* (William Fullbright. *Recent Discoveries in Bible Lands,* p. 136.)

When we put all of this evidence together, we can come to only one conclusion: the New Testament is a historical first-century document that accurately portrays the life of Christ and the lives and works of the apostles. We have available to us today virtually a 100 percent replica of the original text. No other ancient document can claim this kind of verification. No other religion can offer this type of credibility to back up the veracity of its claims and writings.

CHAPTER 10

JESUS CHRIST: GOD INCARNATE

Not only do we believe in the existence of a God, Who is chronicled in accurate, reliable, Scriptural documents, but we also fervently espouse that this God historically revealed Himself over two-thousand years ago in the person of Jesus Christ. Jesus claimed to be the only way to God, equated Himself with God, and said He could forgive sins. He even predicted before His death that He would rise again, which He later fulfilled. In other words, Jesus, in claiming to be God, did everything in a human body you would expect God to do. If Jesus is Who He says He is, He should be listened to and not cavalierly dismissed as a fraud or just a teacher. We must ask the question: "Was Jesus a man of history and did His virgin birth, death on the cross, and bodily resurrection actually occur?" If these events did indeed happen exactly the way the New Testament depicts them, it is then up to the individual to decide, based on the evidence, whether to believe in Christ or reject Him. The spiritual side of Jesus Christ should not be divorced from the historical and physical side. In Christian documents, the spiritual and the historical are inextricably linked together to convey a powerful story of redemption.

Jesus a Man of History

One of the most important facts to establish in our defense of Christianity is that Jesus was a historical person. Over the years, this assertion has been questioned by skeptical scholars, who have reduced Jesus Christ to everything from a myth to a mere mortal who was a victim of his own ambitions but clearly not the Son of God. We know the Bible records Him to be historical, but is there any evidence to support the historicity of Jesus outside of the biblical documents? Many sources do indeed corroborate it. Numerous secular authors who lived during the first century referred to Jesus' life. These witnesses were diverse in occupations and in their opinions about Him. (The following list is compiled from the works of Josh McDowell's, *Evidence That Demands a Verdict*; Bruce Metzger, *New Testament: Its Background, Growth, and Content*; and F.F. Bruce, *The New Testament Documents: Are They Reliable?*.)

Flavius Josephus - first-century Jewish historian

Josephus is perhaps one of the most important historians of the first century. He was a devout Jew in his early life but later turned himself over to the Roman officials through whom he was given privilege to witness firsthand the destruction of the temple in 70 AD. Josephus was deemed a traitor by the Jews but has provided invaluable historical information regarding events in the first century as it related to the Romans and Jews. His two most famous works are entitled *Jewish Antiquities* and *The Jewish War*. Josephus, throughout his writings, verifies many of the biblical characters in the New Testament, both Roman and Jewish. He also substantiates much about Jesus Christ as noted in the following reference:

> *And there arose about this time Jesus, a wise man, if indeed we should call him a man: for he was a doer of marvelous deeds, a teacher of men who receive the truth with pleasure. He led away many Jews, and also many of the Greeks. This man was the Christ. And when Pilate had condemned him to the cross on his impeachment by the chief men among us, those who had loved him at first did not cease; for he appeared to them on the third day alive again, the divine prophets having spoken these and thousands of other wonderful things about him; and even now the tribe of Christians, so named after him, has not yet died out.* (Flavius Josephus, *Jewish Antiquities*. xviii.33)

Cornelius Tacitus - Roman historian, 112 AD

Tacitus was perhaps the greatest of the Roman historians. At about the age of 60, while writing the history of the reign of Nero (54-68AD), he comments on the great fire which did heavy damage to Rome in 64 AD. He relates how it was widely believed that Nero initiated the fire to gain greater glory for himself. Bruce cites Tacitus's reference to Christ and more specifically to His death:

> *Christus, the founder of the name, was put to death by Pontius Pilate, procurator of Judea in the reign of Tiberius; but the pernicious superstition, repressed for a time broke out again.* (F.F. Bruce, *The New Testament Documents: Are They Reliable?*, 71).

Suetonius - Roman historian around 120 AD
Another important Roman historian was Suetonius, secretary to Emperor Hadrian. In about 120 AD, he wrote a famous history called, *The Lives of the Twelve Caesars*. Suetonius made a couple of brief but important references to Christ and Christians:

> *As the Jews were making constant disturbances at the instigation of Chrestus (another spelling of Christus), he expelled them from Rome. Punishment by Nero was inflicted on the Christians, a class of men given to a new and mischievous superstition.*(Josh McDowell, *Evidence That Demands A Verdict,* p.83*)*.

Pliny the Younger - Governor of Bithynia, 112 AD
Pliny the Younger (62 AD - 112 AD) was the governor of Bithynia, a Roman province in Asia Minor. He consulted with Emperor Trajan concerning the line of action he should take against Christians who have been increasing in numbers throughout the province. We know from some of Pliny's communications with Trajan that he had been killing Christians, both men, and children. Metzger elucidates on Pliny's discussion with Trajan, which verifies the historical existence of Christ:

> *A serious economic consequence of their growth was the falling off of the sale of animals designed as sacrificial offering in pagan temples. In a letter written to Trajan about AD 112 (Epis. X.96), Pliny states that the Christians are accustomed to assemble together regularly on a certain day, and "to sing responsively a hymn to Christ as if to a*

> *god."* (Bruce Metzger, *The New Testament, Its Background, Growth, and Content*, pp.76-77)

Lucian of Samosata - Satirist of the second century
Lucian was a satirist of the second century who spoke with distain about Christ and His followers:

> *The man who was crucified in Palestine because he introduced this new cult into the world.... Furthermore, their first lawgiver persuaded then that they were all brothers one of another after they have transgressed once for all by denying the Greek gods and by worshipping that crucified sophist himself and living under his laws.* (cited by Josh McDowell, *Evidence That Demands a Verdict*, p. 82)

Mara Bar Serapion - Letter written sometime after 73 AD to his son
In the British Museum there is a preserved letter written by a Syrian named Mara Bar-Serapion sometime after 73 AD. It was inscribed while he was in prison and was addressed to his son, demonstrating that those who persecuted wise men suffered severe consequences, which included the Jews who executed their King. His letters reads:

> *What advantage did the Athenians gain from putting Socrates to death? Famine and plague came upon them as judgment for their crime. What advantage did the men of Samos gain from burning Pythagoras? In a moment their land was converged with sand. What advantage did*

> *the Jews gain from executing their wise King? It was just after that that their kingdom was abolished.... Nor did the wise King die for good; He lived on in the teaching which He had given.* (F.F. Bruce, *The New Testament, Its Background, Growth, and Content*, p. 114)

Many more examples could be offered to support the historicity of Jesus Christ. However, these extra biblical sources verify the fact that Jesus Christ was not the mere product of some delusional followers who fabricated His story. Jesus was indeed a Person who walked on the pages of history and lived among us.

Jesus an Historical Figure Who Was God

Jesus was not merely a human being Who walked in history; He was also God Who walked in history. This aspect of His Messiahship makes Him very unique among any founder of any other religion. An objective study of His life verifies the fact He was special and accomplished feats unsurpassed by any mere mortal. Scripture unequivocally and emphatically affirms His deity. This man truly was God.

Jesus claimed to be God

Jesus made many claims, the most astounding of which was that He was God:

> *"I tell you the truth," Jesus answered, "before Abraham was born, I am!"* John 8:58

Scholars are in agreement that the use of the phrase *I AM* is a clear reference to Jehovah of the Old Testament. This is the name the God of the Hebrews told Moses to use in identifying Him before Pharaoh.

> *Moses said to God, "Suppose I go to the Israelites and say to them, 'The God of your fathers has sent me to you,' and they ask me, 'What is his name?' Then what shall I tell them?" God said to Moses, "I AM WHO I AM. This is what you are to say to the Israelites: 'I AM has sent me to you.'"* Exodus 3:13-14

The implications of the name *I AM* is that God is the ever present One who guides His people. He was, is, and will ever be. In establishing His credentials of deity, Jesus could claim to exist before Abraham. The next verse records that, after this was said, the Jews tried to stone Him because, in their minds, anyone who claimed to be God was committing blasphemy.

> *"Your father Abraham rejoiced at the thought of seeing my day; he saw it and was glad. You are not yet fifty years old," the Jews said to him, "and you have seen Abraham!" "I tell you the truth," Jesus answered, "before Abraham was born, I am!" At this, they picked up stones to stone him, but Jesus hid himself, slipping away from the temple grounds.* John 8:56-59

In another place Jesus made this statement in regard to His relationship with the Father:

> *I and the Father are one.* John 10:30

Here, He is equating Himself with God. The Jews clearly believed this was the case, because John tells us this was the reason they tried to stone Him:

> *Again the Jews picked up stones to stone him, but Jesus said to them, "I have shown you many great miracles from the Father. For which of these do you stone me?" "We are not stoning you for any of these," replied the Jews, "but for blasphemy, because you, a mere man, claim to be God."* John 10:31-33

Jesus was more than just a fine man or a great teacher. He claimed to be Almighty God. If one makes such a statement, he had better be able to back it up lest he be placed in the category of a deranged fool, fraud or charlatan. The credentials for Jesus' deity are numerous.

Jesus lived as God

If one claims to be God, one should live as God lives: with authority, power and without a sinful blemish. Jesus did this.

He was sinless

Jesus lived a sinless and impeccable life. He passed every moral and ethical test that came His way. Scripture affirms the sinless life of Christ:

> *God made him who had no sin to be sin for us, so that in him we might become the righteousness of God.* 2 Corinthians 5:21

> *He committed no sin, and no deceit was found in his mouth.* 1 Peter 2:22

> *But you know that he appeared so that he might take away our sins. And in him is no sin.* 1 John 3:5

He qualified to be the perfect sacrifice who could take away our sins.

He forgave sins

Only someone who claimed to be God would be able to forgive sins. Jesus demonstrated this prerogative in His ministry:

> *When Jesus saw their faith, he said to the paralytic, "Son, your sins are forgiven."* Mark 2:5

> *"But so that you may know that the Son of Man has authority on earth to forgive sins...." Then he said to the paralytic, "Get up, take your mat and go home."* Matthew 9:6

> *"No one, sir," she said. "Then neither do I condemn you," Jesus declared. "Go now and leave your life of sin."* John 8:11

He demonstrated tremendous power in a variety of arenas

It is reasonable to expect that someone, who claimed to be God, would be able to perform astounding feats. Jesus' demonstration of power in a variety of situations was truly astounding.

- **Healed the sick**
  Jesus performed healings that went far beyond what medicine could accomplish in the first century. They were truly extraordinary healings that defied explanation.

  Jesus reached out his hand and touched the man. "I am willing," he said. "Be clean!" Immediately he was cured of his leprosy. Matthew 8:3

  He said, "Go away. The girl is not dead but asleep." But they laughed at him. After the crowd had been put outside, he went in and took the girl by the hand, and she got up. Matthew 9:24-25

- **Performed astounding miracles**
  Jesus' ministry was marked by outstanding and awe-inspiring miracles. Turning the water into wine was one of them.

  Then he told them, "Now draw some out and take it to the master of the banquet." They did so, and the master of the banquet tasted the water that had been turned into wine. He did not realize where it had come from, though the servants who had drawn the water knew. Then he called the bridegroom aside and said, "Everyone brings out the choice wine first and then the cheaper wine after the guests have had too much to drink; but you have saved the best till now." This, the first of his miraculous signs, Jesus performed at Cana in Galilee. He thus revealed his glory, and his disciples put their faith in him. John 2:8-11

- **Ruled the demonic world**
  As God, Jesus demonstrated superiority and command over the evil forces of Satan. The demons recognized His authority and power as demonstrated in this incident:

  For Jesus had said to him, "Come out of this man, you evil spirit!" Then Jesus asked him, "What is your name?" "My name is Legion," he replied, "for we are many." And he begged Jesus again and again not to send them out of the area. A large herd of pigs was feeding on the nearby hillside. The demons begged Jesus, "Send us among the pigs; allow us to go into them." He gave them permission, and the evil spirits came out and went into the pigs. The herd, about two thousand in number, rushed down the steep bank into the lake and were drowned. Mark 5:8-13

- **Exercised authority and power over nature**
  One would expect that someone who claimed to be God would have authority over nature. On several occasions, Jesus exercised his control over weather forces. The story of Jesus calming the storm on the Sea of Galilee in front of His disciples is vivid example of this:

  He got up, rebuked the wind and said to the waves, "Quiet! Be still!" Then the wind died down and it was completely calm. Mark 4:39

Jesus spoke the greatest words ever spoken

Most revered religious leaders are known for their sage and wisdom reflected in their words, writings and public addresses. Not one person who has ever lived can match the powerful and insightful words of Jesus. He was impressive not only in what He did, but also in what He said. Jesus' words were like no others:

> *They were amazed at his teaching, because his message had authority.* Luke 4:32

> *Heaven and earth will pass away, but my words will never pass away.* Luke 21:33

> *"No one ever spoke the way this man does," the guards declared.* John 7:46

No one in history has been quoted more often than Jesus Christ. What He said and the way He said it revealed the character of God in Him.

He is arguably the most influential Man Who ever lived

Jesus' claim to be God is not only supported by His words, deeds, and proclamations; it is also corroborated by His tremendous impact and influence on the world for 2,000 years. Whether it be in books, songs, schools, art or hospitals, the name of Jesus Christ has impacted the world in a tremendous way. There is not a religious leader that comes close to the effect that Jesus Christ has made on the world for over two-thousand years.

The disciples believed that He was God

Jesus claimed to be God and demonstrated every credential to back up this claim. Furthermore, His disciples, the ones who lived and ministered close by His side for over three years, came to the conclusion that He was God as well. This point is important because, just after His arrest and subsequent crucifixion, they had all left Him in fear and doubt while hiding from the Jewish and Roman authorities. However, something dramatic changed their minds and, after the resurrection, they boldly affirmed the deity of Jesus.

John

John's very first words in his gospel declare unequivocally that Jesus, the Word, was indeed God:

> *In the beginning was the Word, and the Word was with God, and the Word was God.* John 1:1

The Greek construction of the phrase *Word was God* emphasizes Jesus' character and nature. Based on the original language, there is no scholarly way to translate this phrase *a god.* John is clearly intending to identify Jesus as God. The author is equating Jesus with Jehovah of the Old Testament. We know that John is referring to Jesus as the *Word* because, in John 1:14, John indicates that the Word became *flesh.* This is a clear reference to the physical body of Jesus Christ. John unequivocally proclaims in this text that Jesus was indeed God.

John in calling Jesus, the Word, God, follows this up by attributing the creation of the world to Jesus. This clearly supports the idea that Jesus Christ was indeed God.

The idea is also corroborated by Paul in his letter to the Colossians:

> *Through him all things were made; without him nothing was made that has been made.* John 1:3

> *For by him all things were created: things in heaven and on earth, visible and invisible, whether thrones or powers or rulers or authorities; all things were created by him and for him.* Colossians 1:16

Thomas

After the crucifixion of Christ, Thomas would have been the last person to affirm the deity of Christ. He is called "doubting Thomas" for a reason. Even after the disciples came to him and declared that they had seen the risen Christ, Thomas was still incredulous and didn't believe them. However, after Jesus invited Thomas to touch His hands and side (John 20:27), he relented from his posture of unbelief and acknowledged Jesus as his God:

> *Thomas said to him, "My Lord and my God!"* John 20:28

Peter

Peter is remembered as the disciple who denied Jesus Christ three times, because of his doubt concerning his beloved friend to whom he had previously sworn unwavering fidelity and allegiance. Again, Peter is no candidate to declare with passion that Jesus was God. But in his address on the Day of Pentecost, Peter stands up boldly and unabashedly affirms that Jesus Christ was Lord.

> *Therefore let all Israel be assured of this: God has made this Jesus, whom you crucified, both Lord and Christ.* Acts 2:36

> *And everyone who calls on the name of the Lord will be saved.* Acts 2:21

In these verses, the Greek word for *Lord* is *kurios* and is often a reference to Jehovah, the name of God. Jesus demonstrates this use of *kurios* during His repartee with the Pharisees, while answering their question of whose son the Messiah would be. Jesus affirms His deity by quoting Psalms 110:1, where David calls the Messiah Lord (*kurios* in Greek) in the same way he refers to Jehovah as Lord:

> *While the Pharisees were gathered together, Jesus asked them, "What do you think about the Christ? Whose son is he?" "The son of David," they replied. He said to them, "How is it then that David, speaking by the Spirit, calls him 'Lord'? For he says, 'The Lord said to my Lord: Sit at my right hand until I put your enemies under your feet.' If then David calls him 'Lord,' how can he be his son?"* Matthew 22:41-45

There is no question that Jesus adduces Psalm 110:1 use of *kurios* (*Lord*) as proof and evidence that not only was He the Messiah, but God as well. In this regard F.F. Bruce has this to say:

> *Ps.cx. vindicates His right to the title Lord in the sense of ädön, but kurios as henceforth used of Him has a higher dignity even than this; it represents the Ineffable Name of God cf. ver. 21).* (F.F Bruce, *The Acts of the Apostles*, p.96.)

Other verses such as Romans 10:9 and Philippians 2:11, also substantiate that the title *Lord* applied to Jesus and reflected His deity. On the Day of Pentecost, Peter's sermon supports this idea.

Fulfilled prophecy revealed Jesus was God

Although, the New Testament records the events of Jesus' life and ministry on earth, the Old Testament also has much to say about the coming of Christ, the Messiah. Numerous details of Jesus' life were prophesied hundreds of years before He came. The Old Testament clearly anticipated that an anointed Messiah, sent by God, would come and deliver the Jews. This special Messiah was referred to as God in the Old Testament. The name *Immanuel* literally means: *God with us.*

> *Therefore the Lord himself will give you a sign: the virgin will be with child and will give birth to a son, and will call him Immanuel.* Isaiah 7:14

Over 300 distinct details were prophesied in the Old Testament concerning the Messiah, and were fulfilled when Jesus came to earth. No ordinary man's life could have possibly fulfilled so many prophecies. Some would say that this is a coincidence. Perhaps one could construe a scenario of coincidence, if the fulfilled Old-Testament prophecies amounted to a handful. But we are talking of hundreds of events. This is evidence that Jesus was God and was truly the divine Messiah. Here is a sampling of some of the predictions in the Old Testament concerning Christ, literally hundreds of years before the events occurred that were literally fulfilled in His life:

Place of birth would be Bethlehem

We know that Jesus was born in Bethlehem, an event foretold by the ancient prophet Micah several hundred years before the event.

> *But you, Bethlehem Ephrathah, though you are small among the clans of Judah, out of you will come for me one who will be ruler over Israel, whose origins are from of old, from ancient times.* Micah 5:2

New Testament fulfillment:

> *After Jesus was born in Bethlehem in Judea, during the time of King Herod, Magi from the east came to Jerusalem.* Matthew 2:1

Jesus' Lineage

The Old Testament indicates that the Messiah will come from the lineage of David and from the Tribe of Judah.

> *"The days are coming," declares the LORD, "when I will raise up to David a righteous Branch, a King who will reign wisely and do what is just and right in the land."* Jeremiah 23:5

> *You are a lion's cub, O Judah; you return from the prey, my son. Like a lion he crouches and lies down, like a lioness— who dares to rouse him? The scepter will not depart from Judah, nor the ruler's staff from between his feet, until he comes to whom it belongs and the obedience of the nations is his.* Genesis 49:9-10

New Testament fulfillment:

> *Now Jesus himself was about thirty years old when he began his ministry... the son of Amminadab, the son of Ram, the son of Hezron, the son of Perez, the son of Judah....* Luke 3:23, 33

> *A record of the genealogy of Jesus Christ the son of David, the son of Abraham:* Matthew 1:1

Manner of birth

The Old Testament foreshadowed that the Messiah would be born of a woman and the seed of a virgin.

> *And I will put enmity between you and the woman, and between your offspring and hers; he will crush your head, and you will strike his heel.* Genesis 3:15

> *Therefore the Lord himself will give you a sign: the virgin will be with child and will give birth to a son, and will call him Immanuel.* Isaiah 7:14

New Testament fulfillment:

> *All this took place to fulfill what the Lord had said through the prophet: "The virgin will be with child and will give birth to a son, and they will call him Immanuel"—which means, "God with us."* Matthew 1:22-23

> *But when the time had fully come, God sent his Son, born of a woman, born under law.* Galatians 4:4

Jesus' crucifixion

There were many events surrounding His crucifixion which were foreseen in the Old Testament. But two Messianic references stand out: His hands and feet were pierced by nails and He was crucified next to thieves.

> *Dogs have surrounded me; a band of evil men has encircled me, they have pierced my hands and my feet.* Psalms 22:16

> *Therefore I will give him a portion among the great, and he will divide the spoils with the strong, because he poured out his life unto death, and was numbered with the transgressors.* Isaiah 53:12

New Testament fulfillment:

> *So the other disciples told him, "We have seen the Lord!" But he said to them, "Unless I see the nail marks in his hands and put my finger where*

> *the nails were, and put my hand into his side, I will not believe it."* John 20:25

> *Two robbers were crucified with him, one on his right and one on his left.* Matthew 27:38

Events at the cross

Many diverse details transpired during and after the crucifixion of Christ. The Old Testament forecasts that Christ's garments would be torn and cast for lots, and the Romans would offer him vinegar for His thirst.

> *They divide my garments among them and cast lots for my clothing.* Psalms 22:18

> *They put gall in my food and gave me vinegar for my thirst.* Psalms 69:21

New Testament fulfillment:

> *When the soldiers crucified Jesus, they took his clothes, dividing them into four shares, one for each of them, with the undergarment remaining. This garment was seamless, woven in one piece from top to bottom. "Let's not tear it," they said to one another. "Let's decide by lot who will get it." This happened that the Scripture might be fulfilled which said, "They divided my garments among them and cast lots for my clothing." So this is what the soldiers did.* John 19:23-24

> *There they offered Jesus wine to drink, mixed with gall; but after tasting it, he refused to drink it.* Matthew 27:34

Jesus' sayings on the cross

Jesus said many things on the cross. The book of Psalms highlights two of His verbal expressions: the mention of His Father forsaking Him and the final death cry.

> *A psalm of David. My God, my God, why have you forsaken me? Why are you so far from saving me, so far from the words of my groaning?* Psalm 22:1

> *Into your hands I commit my spirit; redeem me, O LORD, the God of truth.* Psalm 31:5

New Testament fulfillment:

> *About the ninth hour Jesus cried out in a loud voice, "Eloi, Eloi, lama sabachthani?"—which means, "My God, my God, why have you forsaken me?"* Matthew 27:46

> *Jesus called out with a loud voice, "Father, into your hands I commit my spirit." When he had said this, he breathed his last.* Luke 23:46

These fulfillments are amazing in themselves. It is impossible to construe a scenario where all of these events could have been planned and orchestrated at an earlier time by Jesus and the disciples.

His burial

The Old Testament foresaw that Jesus' burial would be associated with the grave of a rich man:

> *He was assigned a grave with the wicked, and with the rich in his death, though he had done no violence, nor was any deceit in his mouth.* Isaiah 53:9

New Testament fulfillment:

> *As evening approached, there came a rich man from Arimathea, named Joseph, who had himself become a disciple of Jesus. Going to Pilate, he asked for Jesus' body, and Pilate ordered that it be given to him. Joseph took the body, wrapped it in a clean linen cloth, and placed it in his own new tomb that he had cut out of the rock. He rolled a big stone in front of the entrance to the tomb and went away.* Matthew 27:57-60

Jesus' resurrection

Finally, the Old Testament portends the most important event of all in the life of Jesus: His bodily resurrection.

> *...because you will not abandon me to the grave, nor will you let your Holy One see decay.* Psalm 16:10

New Testament fulfillment:

> *Seeing what was ahead, he spoke of the resurrection of the Christ, that he was not abandoned*

> *to the grave, nor did his body see decay. God has raised this Jesus to life, and we are all witnesses of the fact.* Acts 2:31-32

These fulfilled prophecies are uncanny and can only point to one thing: Jesus Christ was truly God with us.

Jesus: The Resurrected One

The greatest weapon in the defense of Christianity and the most striking evidence of the deity of Christ and His superiority over any other religious leaders, is His bodily resurrection from the dead. The Apostle Paul declares the resurrection from the dead as the key element substantiating that Jesus was the Son of God:

> *...regarding his Son, who as to his human nature was a descendant of David, and who through the Spirit of holiness was declared with power to be the Son of God by his resurrection from the dead: Jesus Christ our Lord.* Romans 1:3-4

No other religious leader has ever predicted that he would be resurrected and later accomplished it. Jesus' resurrection clearly places Him at the top of the religious ladder. He can claim something that no one else can: He arose from the grave and conquered death. There are many aspects of his death and resurrection that are worth examining. They support the truth and factual basis for this incredible event.

Jesus predicted He would rise from the dead

Jesus actually predicted before the event happened that He would resurrect from the dead. He fulfilled this declaration.

> *Jesus answered them, "Destroy this temple, and I will raise it again in three days." The Jews replied, "It has taken forty-six years to build this temple, and you are going to raise it in three days?" But the temple he had spoken of was his body.* John 2:19-20

His resurrection was the basis for the early church's bold witness

When one considers the sense of hopelessness and despondency that descended upon Christs' disciples after His crucifixion, something dramatic had to occur for these dejected, disillusioned followers to ardently and passionately proclaim the victory of Christ. We know that it was the resurrection which turned these hapless men and women into ardent proclaimers of the gospel. The book of Acts gives evidence to this.

> *They were greatly disturbed because the apostles were teaching the people and proclaiming in Jesus the resurrection of the dead.* Acts 4:2

> *For he has set a day when he will judge the world with justice by the man he has appointed. He has given proof of this to all men by raising him from the dead.* Acts 17:31

But I have had God's help to this very day, and so I stand here and testify to small and great alike. I am saying nothing beyond what the prophets and Moses said would happen—that the Christ would suffer and, as the first to rise from the dead, would proclaim light to his own people and to the Gentiles. Acts 26:22-23

All the facts reveal He did not fake His death

- He refused pain-killing drugs; so he was not drugged.

- He had major wounds and hung on the cross all day.

- He suffered brutal beatings and savage floggings before the crucifixion. This kind of devastating torture alone would have killed most men.

- He uttered a death cry.

- He was pierced in His side and blood mixed with water flowed out. The Roman soldiers pronounced Him dead without breaking His legs. They considered this a medical sign of death. These soldiers were professionals in the area of crucifixion and had seen hundreds die this way. It is unlikely they were wrong.

- He was heavily bandaged with about 100 pounds of spices on His body and those doing the embalming recognized that He was not alive.

- Pilate inquired to make sure that Jesus was dead before he gave the body to Joseph of Arimathea.

Theories, such as the body was stolen, are proven false

- There is no indication that Peter and John removed the body from the tomb. They were astonished by what they saw when they looked inside the empty tomb. The Greek language describes the grave clothes as devoid of a body and lay undisturbed as if the body had vaporized (John 20:3-7), proving that a miracle had happened. A live man could not have extricated himself from the grave clothes without disheveling the bandages. Peter and John had no reason to believe beforehand that Christ would arise. This was clearly a supernatural event.

- Joseph of Arimathea did not steal the body. He did not have enough time to do so and there is no indication that he thought Jesus was alive. Why would he have spent time and money preparing the body for burial if he were going to steal it?

- Roman and Jewish authorities did not steal the body since they would have had much to gain by producing the body, thus proving that Jesus had not resurrected, reducing Him to a fraud. In fact, they accused the disciples of stealing the body (Matthew 28:11-15).

- Experienced men heavily guarded the tomb and an official Roman seal was placed around it (Matthew 27:64). The penalty for breaking a Roman seal without authorization was death. The guards would have been executed if they had let someone steal the body.

- The disciples did not steal the body. They were obviously afraid and skeptical. Their lives were on the line if the body was removed and they were not willing to die for a cause they believed was false. Besides, the disciples could not have moved the stone away from the tomb entrance without waking up the guards.

- The women who followed Jesus did not take the body. They knew Jesus well and were convinced that He was still in the tomb. Additionally, how could the women have moved the heavy stone from the tomb entrance and remove the body in front of a Roman guard? The stone was so heavy that tradition says it would have taken several men to move it. The women weren't strong enough to do this.

- The enemies of Christ, from the Romans to the Jewish leadership, could produce no evidence to refute His bodily resurrection from the dead. Truly, the ability to do so would have been much to their advantage. The reason no one could soundly dispute the resurrection of Christ was because of the empty tomb.

- Jesus appeared to many people during the forty days following His resurrection. See 1 Corinthians

15:3-8; Luke 24:33-39; Luke 24:42-43; John 20:26-27.

Without the resurrection of Christ, how do we answer these questions?

- Why couldn't the Jews or Romans produce the body, when it would have been extremely advantageous for the enemies of Christ to do so?

- How do we explain the change in Peter, who had gone from a denier of Christ living in shame and fear, to a bold proclaimer of the gospel on the Day of Pentecost. He did all of this fully knowing he would be persecuted and possibly die for his faith, which history records did eventually happen.

- Why did James, the brother of Christ, suddenly become a follower of the Lord and a leader in the early church (Acts 1:13; 12:17; Galatians 2:9)? Previously, according to the Scriptures, Jesus' family had rejected Him (John 7:5). James is also the author of one of the books in the Bible.

- How do we account for the change in the attitude of the disciples who were willing to die for someone they had previously run from and rejected?

- What is the explanation for how a group of unpretentious disciples could fool the whole world for so long? How do we explain the power of the resurrection for over 2,000 years in the history of mankind? Could a fraud sustain its power for such an enduring period of time?

- Without the resurrection, how do we make sense of the conversion of Paul, a man who had previously hated Christ and persecuted His followers with a vengeance?

- Why did King Agrippa not dispute Paul when he claimed as an historical fact that Jesus had risen from the dead and appealed to Agrippa's knowledge of the event? (Acts 26:22-27)

- How do we account for the exponential growth of the church over the first three centuries when everything from Judaism, the Roman Empire, paganism, and pseudo-Christianity virulently attacked and persecuted her?

- How do we explain the life-changing power of Christianity in individuals as well as in whole societies for thousands of years?

All indications point to the fact that Jesus is God, Who walked in history, accomplishing everything He said he would do, including rising from the dead. If Jesus is God, then He must be listened to. His resurrection makes Christianity tower in stature above any other religion and gives our Lord credentials that exceeds those of any spiritual leader. In this regard, Jesus stands alone.

Truly a Unique Man

To say that Jesus was unique is the greatest understatement of all time. We understand what *unique* means. We use phrases such as *one-of-a kind*, *superstar*, *a phenomenon*, or *someone who comes around once-in-a-lifetime*, to depict such individuals. Whether it is a political leader like Abraham Lincoln or Winston Churchill, an inventor such as Thomas Edison or a mathematical genius personified in Einstein, we know greatness when we see it. But all of the aforementioned individuals pale in comparison to Jesus Christ. The following essay entitled, *The Incomparable Christ*, captures poignantly the uniqueness of this God-man Jesus Christ.

> *More than nineteen hundred years ago there was a Man born contrary to the laws of life. This Man lived in poverty and was reared in obscurity. He did not travel extensively. Only once did He cross the boundary of the country in which He lived; that was during His exile in childhood.*
>
> *He possessed neither wealth nor influence. His relatives were inconspicuous and had neither training nor formal education. In infancy, He startled a king; in childhood He puzzled doctors; in manhood He ruled the course of nature, walked upon the billows as if pavements, and hushed the sea to sleep. He healed the multitudes without medicine and made no charge for His service.*
>
> *He never wrote a book, and yet all the libraries of the country could not hold the books that have*

been written about Him. He never wrote a song, and yet He has furnished the theme for more songs than all the songwriters combined.

He never founded a college, but all the schools put together cannot boast of having as many students.

He never marshaled an army, nor drafted a soldier, nor fired a gun; and yet no leader ever had more volunteers who have, under His orders, made more rebels stack arms and surrender without a shot fired.

He never practiced psychiatry, and yet He has healed more broken hearts than all the doctors far and near. Once each week, the wheels of commerce cease their turning and multitudes wend their way to worshipping assemblies to pay homage and respect to Him.

The names of the past proud statesmen of Greece and Rome have come and gone. The names of the past scientists, philosophers, and theologians have come and gone; but the name of this Man abounds more and more. Though time has spread nineteen hundred years between the people of this generation and the scene of His crucifixion, yet He still lives. Herod could not destroy Him, and the grave could not hold Him.

He stands forth upon the highest pinnacle of heavenly glory, proclaimed of God, acknowledged by angels, adored by saints, and feared by devils, as the living, personal Christ, our

Lord and Savior. (Cited from Josh McDowell, *Evidence That Demands A Verdict,* p135)

CONCLUSION

THE EVIDENCE IS IN: IT'S DECISION TIME

Jesus Christ presents a dilemma to modern man. We cannot glibly dismiss Him from history or write Him off as a myth of delusion. If Jesus existed and was Who He said He was, mankind must decide what to do with Him. It isn't enough to call Him a nice person or a great teacher and yet refuse to acknowledge Jesus as Lord and Savior. C.S. Lewis cogently states:

> *I am trying here to prevent anyone saying the really foolish thing that people often say about Him: "I am ready to accept Jesus as a great moral teacher, but I don't accept His claim to be God." This is the one thing we must not say. A man who was merely a man and said the sort of things Jesus said would not be a great moral teacher. He would either be a lunatic—on a level with the man who says he is a poached egg—or else he would be the Devil of Hell. You must make your choice. Either this man was and is the Son of God: or else a madman or something worse.* (C. S. Lewis. *Mere Christianity*, p. 103.)

There are Three Choices

C.S. Lewis has suggested that there are three choices and conclusions we can come up with regard to Jesus Christ. Let examine each of them:

He was a liar (bad)
One potential conclusion that someone can come to regarding Christ is that He was a liar, whose mendacity and deception reached the level of brilliance. However, if Jesus was a liar, then He was also stupid for allowing Himself to be crucified and killed for a cause in which He did not believe. If He lied, how could we explain that He taught and lived the greatest moral lifestyle the world has ever seen and spoke the greatest words ever uttered? Jesus was even audacious enough to suggest that He was the very paradigm and measurement of truth:

> *Jesus answered, "I am the way and the truth and the life. No one comes to the Father except through me."* John 14:6

> *"You are a king, then!" said Pilate. Jesus answered, "You are right in saying I am a king. In fact, for this reason I was born, and for this I came into the world, to testify to the truth. Everyone on the side of truth listens to me."* John 18:37

Isn't it odd that no one was able to expose Him as a fraud or catch Him in a lie? All information from every source indicates that this Man personified truth and veracity.

He was a lunatic (mad)

One can also draw the conclusion that Jesus was a deluded maniac, as crazy as they come. But, if Jesus was deranged and mentally ill, why did people flock to Him and embrace Him with such enthusiasm and confidence? The common people were not afraid of Jesus. They received His words and welcomed His touch. His life transformed the down and out, the hurting, and the disenfranchised. Jesus even healed those who were mentally unstable and deranged (Mark 5:15). He was calm and in control. His sanity and clear presence of mind are what made Him so attractive. Even as a young man, He was able to discuss, on a high intellectual level, any theological question with the most highly trained scholars and learned people of the day (Luke 1:46-47). He routinely confounded the Jewish lawyers and scribes who sought to trick Him into lying. One has to sink into fantasy to define Jesus as a lunatic. Napoleon, who was prone to criticize organized religion, said this about Jesus:

> *I know men; and I tell you that Jesus Christ is not a man. Superficial minds see a resemblance between Christ and the founders of empires, and the gods of other religions. That resemblance does not exist. There is between Christianity and whatever other religions the distance of infinity.* (Cited by Josh McDowell, *Evidence that Demands a Verdict*, p.106)

C. S. Lewis sums up the problem critics have in trying to explain Jesus Christ apart from the Christian position:

> *The historical difficulty of giving for the life, sayings and influence of Jesus any explanation that*

> *is not harder than the Christian explanation is very great. The discrepancy between the depth and sanity of His moral teaching and the rampant megalomania which must lie behind His theological teaching unless He is indeed God, has never been satisfactorily explained. Hence the non-Christian hypotheses succeed one another with the restless fertility of bewilderment.* (C. S. Lewis. *Miracles*, p. 113)

He was Lord (God)

If Jesus wasn't a liar or a lunatic, the only logical conclusion one can come to about Him is that He is the Lord and Savior that He claimed to be. Our goal in defending our Christian faith is to help people to see the truth and beauty of Jesus Christ and to encourage them to embrace Him as Lord. Committing to Jesus is not to follow a fantasy or a mystical teaching. It is to give one's self to a Person, the Son of God, Who died and rose again. Our prayer should be that as we boldly proclaim Christ, many minds and hearts will be opened to the facts and message of His life and ministry. This is the only hope for our world. That is why the Apostle John wrote:

> *But these are written that you may believe that Jesus is the Christ, the Son of God, and that by believing you may have life in his name.* John 20:31

> *That which was from the beginning, which we have heard, which we have seen with our eyes, which we have looked at and our hands have touched—this we proclaim concerning the Word*

> *of life. The life appeared; we have seen it and testify to it, and we proclaim to you the eternal life, which was with the Father and has appeared to us.* 1 John 1:1-2

If one comes to the conclusion that Jesus Christ is truly Who He said He was, and did indeed bodily rise from the grave, then one must decide on whether to reject Christ's invitation of salvation or receive Him. The choice truly has eternal consequences.

How to Become a Christian

The most important decision any individual makes on this earth is where they will spend eternity. The ultimate goal in defending the Christian faith to the modern world is that men and women will come to know Christ personally. This book is written not only to those who know Christ but also to those who are on a spiritual quest to find the truth about Him. Becoming a Christian is not ultimately about joining a church, reciting creeds, uttering rote and meaningless prayers, knocking on thousands of doors to fulfill a religious quota system, or performing good deeds to earn God's love. Becoming a Christian is about establishing a relationship with God the Father based on a personal commitment and acceptance of Jesus as Lord and Savior. It involves trading our old life with its sin, disappointments, pain, and confusion, for a brand-new life found in knowing the Son of God personally. Two primary components are necessary to become a Christian.

Something to believe

Becoming a Christian involves the head as well as the heart. Faith is built on solid principles of fact and reason, not on emotion and sentimentality. If one wants to become a Christian, one must believe some essential principles:

I am a sinner separated from God

Christianity is built on the premise that man is fundamentally flawed by sin and rebellion. He is not simply misguided or the product of a bad environment. Mankind is sinful at the core and this malady separates him from God the Father. This idea of humanity's depraved condition contradicts the world's idea that everyone is basically good. The Bible vividly describes mankind's fallen state before conversion:

> *All have turned away, they have together become worthless; there is no one who does good, not even one.* Romans 3:12

> *For if, when we were God's enemies, we were reconciled to him through the death of his Son.* Romans 5:10

> *As for you, you were dead in your transgressions and sins, in which you used to live when you followed the ways of this world and of the ruler of the kingdom of the air, the spirit who is now at work in those who are disobedient. All of us also lived among them at one time, gratifying the cravings of our sinful nature and following its desires and thoughts. Like the rest, we were by nature objects of wrath.* Ephesians 2:1-3

They are darkened in their understanding and separated from the life of God because of the ignorance that is in them due to the hardening of their hearts. Ephesians 4:18

In these verses, words such as *worthless*, *darkened*, *enemies*, *dead*, *objects of wrath*, and *separated*, poignantly paint a vivid picture of a person's dire condition before he comes to know Christ. Anyone who becomes a follower of Christ must first of all recognize his sinful condition and unworthiness in the face of a Holy God.

I can never earn a relationship with God

When we recognize our hopeless condition, the next important step is to understand the remedy for this, which is receiving the free gift of God's salvation and forgiveness provided in Christ. This is the main difference between all forms of religion and true Christianity. Most religions focus on human effort to earn a relationship with the Creator. They might say, "Just love more and serve your fellow man." Although these actions are noble and laudable, they are futile in establishing a relationship with God. This connection with God can only be forged through what Jesus Christ did on the cross. This is what is called the "grace of God." Notice what the Bible says:

For it is by grace you have been saved, through faith—and this not from yourselves, it is the gift of God—not by works, so that no one can boast. Ephesians 2:8-9

But when the kindness and love of God our Savior appeared, he saved us, not because of

> *righteous things we had done, but because of his mercy.* Titus 3:4-5

I must believe the facts of the gospel

Once I understand my wretched condition before God and that I cannot rectify this through human effort, I must now come to personally accept and believe the good news (gospel) of what Christ has accomplished. Paul defines this gospel in 1 Corinthians 15:1-4:

> *Now, brothers, I want to remind you of the gospel I preached to you, which you received and on which you have taken your stand. By this gospel you are saved, if you hold firmly to the word I preached to you. Otherwise, you have believed in vain. For what I received I passed on to you as of first importance: that Christ died for our sins according to the Scriptures, that he was buried, that he was raised on the third day according to the Scriptures, and that he appeared to Peter, and then to the Twelve. After that, he appeared to more than five hundred of the brothers at the same time, most of whom are still living, though some have fallen asleep. Then he appeared to James, then to all the apostles, and last of all he appeared to me also, as to one abnormally born.* 1 Corinthians 15:1-8

Paul specifically declares that this salvation gospel whereby we are saved has some key components:

1. Christ died for our sins.

2. Christ was buried.

3. Christ was raised from the dead on the third day.

All of these components provide the foundation for our salvation. There is no other way to God except through acknowledging and embracing the finished work of Jesus Christ.

The Bible has good news for all of mankind. Jesus has done everything necessary to provide salvation. Christianity may be free to us but it came at a costly price: the death of Jesus. Every sin that mankind had ever committed or ever would commit was placed on the back of God's Son as He hung on the cross. His blood paid the price for our sin. This good news is called the *gospel.* Faith in Christ simply means that I accept (without qualification) that His death for my sins, burial, and resurrection from the grave are not only historically accurate but form the basis for my coming to God. On this subject Scripture is clear:

> *For God so loved the world that he gave his one and only Son, that whoever believes in him shall not perish but have eternal life.* John 3:16

> *Jesus answered, "I am the way and the truth and the life. No one comes to the Father except through me."* John 14:6

> *They replied, "Believe in the Lord Jesus, and you will be saved—you and your household."* Acts 16:31

> *We are therefore Christ's ambassadors, as though God were making his appeal through us. We implore you on Christ's behalf: Be reconciled to God. God made him who had no sin to be sin for us, so that in him we might become the righteousness of God.* 2 Corinthians 5:20-21

Becoming a Christian is so simple that it seems too easy. Christ has finished the work of salvation. One of the last things that Jesus said before He died was, "It is finished." All that mankind has to do to be saved and to establish a relationship with the God of the Bible is to accept by faith, the free gift of God's love through Christ. Faith, in biblical terms, is not a merely a mental assent but an embracing and commitment to that which is believed upon.

To illustrate this point, there is a story of a crowd watching a man sitting on a unicycle getting ready to cross a high wire. Someone asked the crowd, "How many of you believe that the man on the unicycle can cross the wire safely?" Everyone raised their hand affirmatively. Then the crowd was asked, "How many of you believe he can cross the wire on a unicycle with a chair in his hand?" The crowd again unanimously raised their hands. Then the question was asked, "How many of you believe this man can cross the wire on a unicycle with a person sitting in the chair?" Without missing a beat, all of the crowd enthusiastically raised their hands expressing their faith in the man on the high wire. Then the question was posed to the crowd, "Which one of you wants to get in the chair?" No one raised their hand. Faith in Christ simply means we are willing to get in the chair that Jesus is holding for the rest of our lives.

Someone to receive

Becoming a Christian not only involves *believing something*, but also *receiving someone*. When one becomes a Christ follower, he embraces a certain set beliefs. However, becoming a Christian involves much more than a mental endorsement or assent to a set of historical facts; it also encompasses a commitment to Jesus Himself. There are a couple of important points here.

Salvation is a personal relationship with Jesus Christ

Jesus called people to receive Him personally. He invited individuals to embrace Him spirit, soul, and body as Lord and Savior, and to follow Him even if it might lead to their death. In essence, He called for their worship and unfailing loyalty and adoration. Notice how the disciples worshipped Him when He appeared to them after His resurrection:

> *Suddenly Jesus met them. "Greetings," he said. They came to him, clasped his feet and worshiped him.* Matthew 28:9

For the rest of our lives we give Him all that we *were*, all that we *are*, and all that we *will be*. Becoming a Christian is a total surrender to Christ, spirit, soul and body. Christianity is ultimately a *relationship* with Christ, not a dead *religion* full of rules and regulations. The Bible is unequivocal that salvation involves making a total commitment of our lives to Jesus. This is truly what it means to believe in Him. Jesus expressed this idea to His disciples when He declared Himself as the "Bread of Life". He stressed the necessity of them feeding on Him:

> *Then Jesus declared, "I am the bread of life. He who comes to me will never go hungry, and he who believes in me will never be thirsty."* John 6:35

In a similar fashion, during His conversation with the woman at the well, Jesus uses the metaphor of water from a well to illustrate that those who follow Him must drink from His water to experience a permanent solution to spiritual thirstiness:

> *Jesus answered, "Everyone who drinks this water will be thirsty again, but whoever drinks the water I give him will never thirst. Indeed, the water I give him will become in him a spring of water welling up to eternal life."* John 4:13-14

Perhaps the greatest illustration of the close and affectionate bond between Christ and His followers is that of a marriage relationship. The Bible declares that to truly know Jesus means that we become His bride and participate in a loving and adoring relationship with Him for the rest of eternity.

> *I am jealous for you with a godly jealousy. I promised you to one husband, to Christ, so that I might present you as a pure virgin to him.* 2 Corinthians 11:2

> *Husbands, love your wives, just as Christ loved the church and gave himself up for her.* Ephesians 5:25

Committing to Jesus means a willingness to follow Him

Earlier, when we discussed the differences between Christianity and all other religions, we stated that one of the distinctions was that Christianity placed the emphasis on the worship of Jesus first, before the adherence to His teachings. However, the byproduct of knowing Christ personally is also to be willing to follow His instructions and teachings. One of Jesus' final instructions to His disciples was to go to the world and preach the gospel, while making disciples and admonishing others to follow His teachings and commandments:

> *Therefore go and make disciples of all nations, baptizing them in the name of the Father and of the Son and of the Holy Spirit, and teaching them to obey everything I have commanded you. And surely I am with you always, to the very end of the age.* Matthew 28:19-20

In Luke 6:46, Jesus even stressed the importance of His followers doing what He said, *"Why do you call me, 'Lord, Lord,' and do not do what I say?"* As a Christian, our lives are to be a reflection of everything He said and did when He walked this earth. We are to exhibit His incredible love for the lost and each other, His commitment to purity and holiness, His focus on prayer and worship of the Father, the incredibly powerful dimensions of the Kingdom of Heaven prevalent throughout His ministry, and a willingness to preach the gospel of Christ to all who will listen.

Are you willing to say this prayer?
This book has a two-fold purpose:

1. To strengthen the faith of Christians and to offer them a pathway for sharing the message of Christ with confidence, to a critical and unbelieving world.

2. To offer sensible answers for honest skeptics of Christianity who have a genuine interest in the Son of God. The upshot being that they would find Christ as their personal Savior. In his wonderful book, *Basic Christianity*, John Stott offers a prayer for honest seekers of Christianity to pray during their journey of investigation. I invite anyone who has read this book and is honestly seeking for the truth about Christ, to pray this prayer:

   God if you exist (and I don't know if you do), and if you hear this prayer (and I don't know if you can), I want to tell you that I am an honest seeker after the truth. Show me if Jesus is your Son and the Savior of the world. And if you bring conviction to my mind, I will trust him as my Savior and follow him as my Lord. (John Stott, *Basic Christianity*, p.19)

I believe if you have uttered this prayer, God will respond to it. If you have found Christ as your Savior, or have further questions, please email me at lesbmri@hotmail.com.

APPENDIX 1

ANSWERING THE TOUGH QUESTIONS

Non-Christians will often ask honest questions regarding our faith in Christ. It is important that we make an attempt to answer them. The following are 25 common questions a Christian will be asked by unbelievers. If one can answer these questions, he will be able to present effectively the defense of his faith.

Question #1 - All religions are good; why advocate only Christianity as the way to God? Isn't this arrogant and narrow-minded?

Answer: We are not implying that all religions are bad or devoid of anything meaningful and helpful. What we are saying is that Christianity exceeds all religions in presenting a comprehensive explanation of life that includes God, creation, sin, man, and life after death. We are also stating that whenever Christianity and other religions differ in doctrine and related issues, Christianity will be the accepted position. We also believe that the founder of Christianity, Jesus Christ, has greater credentials over all other religious leaders because of His resurrection from the dead. Christianity, by its nature, is exclusive just as any truth is. Therefore, we should not apologize if we appear narrow-minded, since Jesus Himself was narrow-minded in stating He was the only way to God.

Question#2 - Why should I become a Christian when there are so many hypocrites?

Answer: When we talk about hypocrisy, we imply that there is a true and decent standard by which we can measure something. Hypocrisy cannot exist unless something ideal and pure exists. It is true that many Christians are hypocrites and do not live up to what Jesus Christ is all about. We must remember that He is the true standard. It makes no difference how many hypocrites there are; mankind still must make a decision about Christ. Furthermore, hypocrites appear in every walk of life. There are hypocrites in the medical, teaching, government, judicial, and law-enforcement fields. The hypocrites do not negate or discredit the individuals who truly represent their fields with truth and dignity. It is a logical fallacy to use one or two bad examples as representation of all.

It is also important to note that most people who use the "hypocrite defense" for not following Christ are looking for an excuse to avoid facing their own faults and sins. However, someday those who have rejected Christ will stand before the judgment seat of God and be held accountable for their own decisions. The Lord will judge them based not on the hypocrites they witnessed, but for their own personal rejection of Christ. Yes, there are many Christian hypocrites on this planet. Not everyone who claims to be a Christian truly is one at heart. But it is also true is that there are millions of devout and exemplary followers of Jesus Christ all over the world who walk the talk of their faith.

Question #3 - Isn't Christianity all psychological? Don't people believe in God because they need to, not because He really exists?

Answer: This is an assumption that many atheists and skeptics of God try to make. However this is not necessarily true of everyone. Some people may believe in God because of the subjective reason it makes them feel good, but this is not the general rule. After all, over 95% of the people on this planet believe in some form of god or Supreme Being. There are valid, logical reasons for the belief in the existence of God. We could reverse this question and say, "Those who do not believe in God are totally illogical, relying only on their feelings and emotions in rejecting God." Christians believe in God because the world makes no sense without Him. The evidence points to a God Who exists outside of any fantasies or emotions.

Question #4 - Isn't the Bible full of errors, making it unreliable?

Answer: The skeptic who asks this question has made assumptions that he has probably never researched. Here is where we should invite the critic to offer specific examples of his charges. Usually they cannot produce any. There are some apparent inconsistencies in the Bible that are hard to explain but generally, logical explanations exist for such seeming inconsistencies. We must admit that we are at a disadvantage in fully understanding a document written over 3500 years ago. Over a century ago, hundreds of biblical contradictions and factual errors were alleged. Today, because of the discoveries of archaeology and the abundant availability of early biblical manuscripts, these contradictions have been reduced to single numbers. The

Bible is totally reliable and verifiable. If someone impugns the accuracy of the Bible because of alleged errors, we need to require them to be scholarly about their own position and offer specific examples to support their claims and then attempt to answer their questions and assertions.

Question #5 - How can a loving God allow so much evil in the world?

Answer: In a seemingly strange way, evil is the result of God's love. God loved Adam so much that He gave him freedom of choice: the freedom to do or not to do what God asked of him. God allows evil because man brought it to this planet through his choices. Also, a powerful evil force called "the devil" exists. He has a vast army of helpers that assist him in concocting many schemes that he employs to keep this planet in a mess. God loved this earth so much that He sent His Son, Jesus Christ, to provide the answer for all of the evil in this world. It is often through the pain and suffering of this planet that mankind will reach out to a loving and life-giving God. The Christian has an explanation for the origin and continued manifestation of evil. The non-Christian is faced with the same question concerning evils origin and existence. Unfortunately, he has little resources or foundation to explain it. One day, when Jesus Christ finally returns, all evil, pain and suffering will be eliminated from the earth.

Question #6 - Why are there so many different translations and versions of the Bible? Doesn't this prove biblical inconsistency?

Answer: This is a trick question. There is a difference between the original manuscripts of the Bible and translations and versions of it. The original biblical manuscripts were written primarily in Hebrew and Greek and focus on the original transmission of the document. On the other hand, translations present the meaning of the original in the native language of the people with whom the translation is trying to communicate. For instance, the original might say, "Jesus the man". The translation in French, Spanish, or Russian might translate the original as, "Jesus the person", or "Jesus the individual". Both would be acceptable. It is no different than reading an English translation of *Les Miserables* which was originally written in French. There may be subtle differences between the French and English versions, but the main ideas come across clearly.

Different translations of the Bible effect no major doctrines germane to biblical Christianity. The Bible is unequivocal, regardless of the translation, in its teachings concerning the divinity, virgin birth, vicarious death on the cross, and resurrection of Christ. It is also unambiguous in declaring that salvation is only attained by faith in the finished work of Christ on the cross. Remember, those who offer the translation or interpretation excuse are generally those who have never carefully studied the Bible. Make the questioner come up with the specific translation difficulty he is referring to. Most of the time he cannot.

Question #7 - Why can't we accept Jesus as just a good, moral teacher and not the Son of God?

Answer: To say that Jesus is a good moral teacher and, at the same time, deny that He is the Son of God is to call Him a liar and a fraud. Jesus' moral teachings and His wisdom cannot be divorced from His claims to be God, to forgive sins, and execute final judgment on the earth. All of His claims are true or none of His claims are true. One cannot have it both ways. One is not considered moral, ever in our day, if He is an inveterate liar.

Question #8 - If God exists, who created Him?

Answer: This question presents the ultimate conundrum. The answer is that no one created God. He is the *uncaused cause* that existed from eternity. There has to be a place where something uncaused is responsible for the creation. Whether one is a theist or an atheist, both have to accept the fact that something existed from eternity to create our world. The Christian believes that this view fits the description of God, while the non-theist must have some cataclysmic event or non-personal force such as the "big bang theory" to account for the creation. If one accepts the fact that there is an uncaused cause responsible for all of creation, including man, the ultimate issue is what does one do with this Creator, not who created Him?

Question #9 - What about the non-Christian who has never heard of Jesus? A loving God would not judge such people.

Answer: The Scripture is clear that God's existence is self-evident in this world. Romans chapter 1, declares that mankind is without excuse. God can be known. Anyone who wants to know God will be able to discover Him. Any person on planet earth can look at the stars and realize that there is someone intelligent out there Who created them. All he has to do is seek and ask for the Creator to reveal Himself. Most of the world is not even responding to natural revelation available for all to see. Instead, many people in the world worship numerous inferior gods in many forms. Remember, the person who asks the question about the heathen has generally heard about Jesus. When he stands before God, the Lord will not ask him about everyone else. He or she will be responsible for the level of revelation they have received about Christ. We do know that God is just and a "Righteous Judge", and He always does things right with His creation. Therefore, however He deals with the lost who have never heard about Jesus, will be fair and equitable.

Question #10 - If one cannot prove God exists, why should I believe in His existence?

Answer: Proof really can only be ascertained by observing data. Most of us live in a world of probabilities, not certainties. We, as well as the Christian skeptic, believe many things we have not seen. History is believed, not because we have personally witnessed everything, but because we believe in sources that present a high degree of probability that something or someone existed or that an event happened. Modern man believes in many things he cannot see or prove. Faith is a reasonable position based on probability. The Christian asserts that an abundance of evidence provides a high degree of probability that the Supreme Being, Whom we call God, actually exists. Faith in the existence of God is ultimately a matter of the heart based on the evidence available. It requires more faith ***not*** to believe in God, that to believe in Him.

Question #11 - Why should I become a Christian when history records murderous acts in the name of Christ? Isn't Christianity historically violent?

Answer: This question is easy to answer. We don't justify killing in the name of Christianity. It is true that, in the past, religious zealots who have claimed to be Christians have killed innocent people. Some abuses during the Crusades and the inquisitions historically bear this out. The Reformation was rife with heinous acts perpetrated by those who claimed to represent the church. Even today, there are also some fringe lunatic movements, who claim to represent Christ, that advocate violence. These are anecdotal examples, and do not represent the vast majority of Christian believers.

On the contrary, it is also true that Christians with their message of God's love in Christ have saved untold millions of lives and are responsible for a moral environment in many nations that prevented needless death and destruction. All who claim to be Christians are not Christians! True followers of Christ do not purposely murder innocent people in His name. There are also many examples in history of pacifists and peacemakers who claimed the name of Christ. We must go back to one of Jesus' teachings, "Blessed are the peacemakers." Jesus led the most historic and world changing revolution that history has ever witnessed without firing a bullet or killing anyone. Real and authentic Christianity must be assessed on the life and teachings of Jesus, not on the violent charlatans and imitators who claim to be His followers.

Question #12 - Isn't Christianity and true science contradictory?

Answer: Christianity and science are not contradictory but complementary. Many of the greatest scientists of history embraced the idea of God, believing that the world of order had to have a Creator. Learned men of science like Kepler, Newton, Pascal, Boyle, Faraday, and Marconi are only a few of the famous scientists who embraced a theistic position. Numerous scientists around the globe in various scientific fields embrace a theistic position. Christianity is not opposed to science, but is hostile to the "religion of science", which has no room for God in its worldview. Often, science seeks to explain everything by natural methods, while denigrating any other position which might contradict or disprove its presuppositions. This is not true science but the religion of science. True science makes sense only when we realize that the complexities of design in the universe suggest an intelligent designer. Francis Schaeffer quotes from Francis Bacon expressing his high view of religion and faith:

> *Man by the fall fell at the same time from his state of innocence and from his dominion over creation. Both of these losses, however, can even in this life be in some parts repaired, the former by religion and faith, the latter by arts and sciences.* (Francis Schaeffer, *How Should We Then Live?* pp. 132-133)

Question #13 - I am a good person; why do I need God to go to heaven?

Answer: Someone once said, "Good people don't go to heaven; perfect people do." Fundamental to Christian theology is the fact that all of mankind is flawed with a sin condition. Since we are dealing with a perfect God, it takes perfection to satisfy Him. Sin and God are incompatible. This is where Jesus comes in. He was the perfect sacrifice for our sins. He was the only human Who could satisfy God's demand for perfection. When we receive Christ, God imputes Jesus' perfection to us, thus allowing us to have a relationship with a Holy God. This according to Scripture, is the only way to heaven. Good doesn't cut it. Besides, how would we ever know when were we're doing good enough?

Question #14 - Isn't the possibility of a person's rising from the dead ridiculous?

Answer: This viewpoint is true only in a worldview where miracles cannot happen. Many skeptics beg the question by stating it is impossible for miracles to occur. This predisposition closes them off from fair historical analysis. The resurrection of Christ is a part of history and is one of the most verifiable events of antiquity. The Christian believes in a supernatural world that has been active in history. One should not attack the veracity of the resurrection of Christ from the dead, when he has not taken time to research this historical event and the primary documents that attest to it.

Question #15 - Aren't people who follow Christianity in reality ignorant, gullible, and naive?

Answer: This view falsely assumes that all Christians have blindly accepted Christ without reason or logic. Many brilliant persons in all disciplines of life, from science, music, art and mathematics, have embraced the Christian faith. Christianity is a faith based on a rational, factual, and intellectually sound foundation. Ultimately, the heart determines the decision, not gullibility, lack of intelligence or insufficient facts.

Question #16 - Wasn't the Bible written too many years ago to be accurate today?

Answer: The reliability and accuracy of historical documents should be based on scientific evidence, not on a biased hunch. Though inscribed in the first century, the biblical documents have been demonstrated as reliable because of the abundance of early manuscripts available and the plethora of outside witnesses who lived during the first two centuries of the church. Those who study manuscripts assert that we have a copies of about 99.5 percent of the original manuscripts of the New Testament. Findings such as the Dead Sea Scrolls and the witness of ancient voices concerning the meticulous nature with which the Jewish scribes preserved their Scriptures, attest to the accuracy of the Old Testament manuscripts. The prodigious amount of archaeology verifications and the amazing number of fulfilled prophecies also lend support to the accuracy of the Scriptures.

Question #17 - Isn't God too loving to send people to eternal damnation?

Answer: It isn't love or lack of love that determines eternal judgment. Ones future destiny is determined by his acceptance of and belief in Jesus Christ (John 3:16). John affirms that those who have the Son have life and those who do not know the Son do not have life (I John 5:11-12). It was God's love that sent His only Son to the cross so that mankind would not be condemned (John 3:16-18). God's love allows men and women to make the decision to reject or to accept His Son. Furthermore, God is just. Because all of mankind outside of Christ stands guilty before Him, He cannot allow anyone to have a relationship with Him nor allow anyone into heaven unless they have been declared "not guilty" by the blood of Christ. The book of Revelation makes it clear that at the final judgment one must be in the Lamb's book of life to spend eternity with the Lord:

> *Then death and Hades were thrown into the lake of fire. The lake of fire is the second death. If anyone's name was not found written in the book of life, he was thrown into the lake of fire.* Revelation 20:14-15

Question #18 - Why should I become a Christian when I know some believers who have more problems than I have?

Answer: All Christians and non-Christians have problems. The issue isn't how many problems one has, but whether one has a personal relationship with Jesus Christ, the One Who can solve those problems. We come to Christ with a lot of sinful issues. It is in coming to Christ that we have a way to deal with our faults. The Christian life is a lifetime process whereby the Lord begins to help us with our issues and difficulties. Every person is held individually responsible before God. To reject Christ because some other person, who is a Christian, has problems will not alter God's plan or excuse our own personal responsibility in this area. We are judged based on our own sins and our own life, not someone else's.

Question #19 - If Jesus was so innocent, great and powerful, why did they kill Him? Why didn't He stop them?

Answer: Christ was killed because His life and message threatened the political and religious culture of His day, not because He was a criminal or a fraud. Many great people have been killed because they spoke the truth or challenged the evil in their society. Martin Luther King was murdered because he stood for what was right and just. Jesus even said that many of His followers would be killed. This happens because the message of Christ is true and right, and contradicts many of the secular philosophies and moral degradations of our society. Also, the purpose of Christ coming to earth was to die for the sins of the world. He was not a victim but a willful participant in His own death, that had been planned long before it happened (John 10:15-18). Scripture also declares it was God's will for Him to die (Acts 4:27-28).

Question #20 - Isn't science more accurate than the Bible and more reliable in explaining the meaning of life?

Answer: This viewpoint is what many in the modern scientific community want us to believe. This is where science has often usurped the role of religion in explaining the meaning of life and has, in essence, become a religion unto itself. Thousands of top scientists around the world are ***theists*** and hold to a "special-creation theory" of the universe or to an "intelligent design" model which necessitates that some personal force other than chance made the universe. God is the Creator of science and life. Therefore, true science, (without bias or preconceived notions) is in harmony with the Bible. It is important that science leave matters related to God, the origin of life, and eternal matters in the hands of faith, not a laboratory.

Question #21 - Miracles belong to religion, not history. Why believe in miracles when they can't be verified?

Answer: At least one historical miracle has been attested to by primary sources: the resurrection of Christ from the dead. Christ's resurrection is a part of history and has been recorded as such. When looked at objectively, the resurrection of Christ is one of the most documented events that has ever occurred. Four primary witnesses, recorded in the four gospels, chronicled the event and others close to the time of the resurrection, such as Luke and Paul, attest to the authenticity of the resurrection of Christ. Those who deny the historical validity of the resurrection, have a hard time explaining the dramatic change in the disciples, the conversion of Paul, and the exponential growth of the early church that was bathed in the blood of the martyrs. The impact of Christianity for two-thousand years worldwide is a testimony to the historical reliability of Christ's resurrection.

We should not allow critics of the resurrection to get away with their skepticism when they have not analyzed the facts and the truth. It is illogical to deny the existence of a miracle of this nature by simply stating it cannot exist, therefore refusing to verify or look at any historical analysis of the occurrence which might prove the negative assertion as inaccurate.

Question #22 - If all of Jesus' works and miracles really happened, how come the whole world doesn't believe in Him?

Answer: Becoming a Christian is ultimately about faith. Evidence alone is not the reason that people believe in Christ. Many first-century witnesses saw His miracles (including the resurrection of Lazarus from the dead) and still sought to kill Him. Jesus was a threat to His culture and to the legalistic religion of the Jews. He confronted man's selfishness and evil heart. The Lord rejected religion that abused and exploited its followers. Jesus called mankind to a higher level of living that placed God at the center of the universe, not man. If one does not want to deal with his heart and his sin, he will reject Christ in spite of the facts.

Question #23 - I know people in other religions who live more exemplary lives than some Christians live. Why then become a Christian?

Answer: The message of Christianity is not that good people need to come to Jesus but that all humans are flawed sinners in need of a Savior. Scripture declares that all have sinned and all have fallen short of God's standards (Romans 3:23). All are dead in sins and trespasses. We cannot know God unless Christ has washed us totally clean and given us a right standing before God. It is perfection, not goodness that is necessary to have a relationship with God. Perfection only comes through Christ. Many atheists and non-Christians live exemplary lives, but reject Christ. The ultimate issue is whether one knows Christ and has been cleansed and declared righteous by His blood, not whether he lives a good life. Christianity is founded on the grace of God, not the good works and deeds of man (Ephesians 2:8-9).

Question #24 - If Christianity is so superior, how do you explain the rapid growth of other religions?

Answer: Size does not equal authenticity, reliability, truth, or soundness. Hitler had huge followings and large crowds listening to his every word, yet he was clearly evil and wrong. Cults and new age religious groups that oppose the historic Christian faith have experienced sizeable growth over the years. Deception is powerful. Also, Satan has a formidable and vast control over many religions opposed to Christ. Most people are religious or desire some religion that gives them a compass outside of themselves. This desire means they might seek psychics or other religious substitutes that are opposed to the message of Christ. Remember, the ultimate test is the founder of the religion. Jesus is superior to all other religious leaders. Therefore, the size of other religions is irrelevant.

Question #25 - Isn't it impossible to be certain if Christianity is true? How do we know for sure the Christian message isn't a hoax?

Answer: The real question is, "How do we know that anything is true?" If we apply to Christianity and the Bible the standards for determining truth we apply to other aspects of life, we will find that the Christian faith is true and meets the standards of truth. There is a double standard often applied here because often, critics of Christianity have not done due diligence in researching and examining the evidence available to them. An objective evaluation of Christianity based on the facts and the research leads to a very credible historical affirmation of the Christian faith.

SCRIPTURE INDEX

Old Testament

SUBJECT INDEX

BIBLIOGRAPHY

Albright, William F. *The Archaeology of Palestine*. Baltimore: Johns Hopkins University Press, 1956.

___. *Recent Discoveries in Bible Lands*. New York: Funk and Wagnalls, 1955.

Archer, Gleason. *A Survey of Old Testament Introduction*. Chicago: Moody Press, 1964.

Bruce, F. F. *The New Testament Documents: Are They Reliable?* Grand Rapids: Eerdmans Publishing, 1960.

___. *The Defence of The Gospel*. Grand Rapids: Eerdmans Publishing, 1959.

___. *The New International Commentary on the New Testament: Hebrews*. Grand Rapids: Eerdmans Publishing, 1964.

___. *The Acts of the Apostles*. Grand Rapids: Eerdmans Publishing, 1951. Rapids: Eerdmans Publishing, 1964.

Eusebius . *Ecclesiastical History*. Grand Rapids: Baker Book House, 1973.

Finegan, Jack: *Encountering New Testament Manuscripts*. Grand Rapids: Eerdmans Publishing Company, 1974.

Geisler, Norman. *Christian Apologetics*. Grand Rapids: Baker, 1976.

Geisler, Norman & Nix, William. *A General Introduction to the Bible*. Chicago: Moody Press, 1968.

Glueck, Nelson. *Rivers in the Desert: History of the Negev*. Philadelphia: Jewish Publications Society of America, 1969.

Greenlee, Harold. *Introduction to New Testament Textual Criticism*. Grand Rapids: Eerdmans Publishing Company, 1964.

Greenslade, Stanley Lawrence (ed.). *Cambridge History of the Bible*. New York: Cambridge University Press, 1963.

Harrison, R.K. *Introduction to the Old Testament*. Grand Rapids: Eerdmans Publishing Company, 1969.

Josephus, Flavius. *Jewish Antiquities and The Jewish War*.

Lane, David. *Reasonable Faith*. Wheaton: Crossway, 2008.

Lewis, C. S. *Mere Christianity*. London: G. Blies, 1945.

___. *Miracles*. New York: Macmillan, 1947.

___. *God in the Dock*. Grand Rapids: Eerdmans, 1970

___. *The Problem of Pain*. New York: The Macmillan Company, 1962.

MacArthur, John. *The MacArthur New Testament Commentary: Romans 1-8*. Chicago: The Moody Bible Institute, 1991.

McDowell, Josh. *Evidence That Demands a Verdict*. San Bernardino: Here's Life Publishers, 1986

___. *Answers To Tough Questions*. San Bernardino: Here's Life Publishers, 1983.

Metzger, Bruce. *The New Testament: Its Background, Growth, and Content*. Nashville: Abingdon Press, 1965.

___. The Text of the New Testament. New York: Oxford University Press, 1968.

Montgomery, John Warwick, ed. *Evidence for Faith*. Dallas: Probe Books, 1991.

___. *History and Christianity*. Downers Grove: InterVarsity Press, 1975.

___. *Sensible Christianity*. (Tape series) 1984.

Morris, Henry. *Many Infallible Proofs*. San Diego: Creation-Life Publishers, 1974.

Ramsay, Sir William. *ST. PAUL the Traveller and the Roman Citizen*. Grand Rapids: Baker Book House, 1962.

Rienecker, Fritz. *Linguistic Key to the Greek New Testament.* Grand Rapids: The Zondervan Publishing House, 1976.

Rushdoony, R. J. *The Necessity for Creationism* (Pamphlet). Pasadena: Jotham Productions.

Schaeffer, Francis. *The God Who Is There*. Downers Grove: InterVarsity Press, 1968.

___. *Genesis in space and time.* Downers Grove: InterVarsity Press, 1972.

___. *How Should We Then Live*. Wheaton: Crossway Books, 1976.

Stott, John. *Basic Christianity*. Downers Grove: Inter-Varsity Press, 1971.

Unger, Merrill. *Archaeology and the Old Testament.* Grand Rapids: Zondervan Publishing House, 1962.

Zecharias, Ravi. *Can Man Live Without God?* Dallas: Word Publishing, 1994.

WEBSITES

www. abcnews.go.com

www.answeringenesis.org

PERIODICALS

Christian Research Journal, Vol 27, number 2, 2004.

Saturday Evening Post, Nov/Dec, 1999

ConTact - Jody Foster

CPSIA information can be obtained
at www.ICGtesting.com
Printed in the USA
BVHW060246040120
568494BV00009B/124/P

9 781545 603727